# Wine Stories : A Little Sip of Italy

# Wine Stories : A Little Sip of Italy

Elizabeth Calhoun

ISBN 10: 1539594718
ISBN 13: 9781539594710
Library of Congress Control Number: 2016917558
CreateSpace Independent Publishing Platform
North Charleston, South Carolina

Printed by CreateSpace, An Amazon.com Company
eStore address: www.CreateSpace.com/6034098
CreateSpace, Charleston SC

*To Bacchus, Edesia, and Hedone, for their inspiration*
*To lovers of wine, food, and travel*
*To love*
*and*
*To Italy*

# Table of Contents

# *Prologue*

I DREAMED OF Tuscany, and Italy, as other children dreamed of Disneyland.

Italy has always fascinated me—the history, the food, the wine, the diverse geography—perhaps because of the stories my grandfather told me about Italy. As Italy was rising out of the ashes of World War II, he had been stationed at Camp Darby, near the town of Livorno, in the region of Tuscany. It was there that he found the love of his life, Sophia. He brought her back to America with him.

I never heard my nonna's stories, as she died not long after I was born, but I know her Italian blood runs in my veins, and her Italian spirit shapes my character. And because of his love for her, and Italy, Grandfather carried on many traditions of the Italian home, including wonderful food and almost always wine with dinner. With his encouragement, I, too, came to appreciate wine, Italy, and all things Italian.

My grandparents never traveled back to Italy, constrained by finances and the demands of the farm and work and family. But I could occasionally get Grandfather to tell me a story or two about his time there.

I found myself particularly drawn to Tuscany, my grandmother's birthplace. It seemed a magical place, with golden sunlight pouring onto green hills topped with towns out of a Renaissance painting. I daydreamed over Italian paintings and photos and travel guides. I read histories and came to know the de Medici family, Michelangelo, and da Vinci. As I grew up, I frequented Italian restaurants, bought cookbooks, and came to know a little about Italian wines, searching wine shops for new and different wines to try. I even had an Italian boyfriend, Giotto.

After I graduated from college, Grandfather offered to send me to Italy. I asked if he might come along with me, but he declined. His health, he said. But I perceived that he might have other reasons as well. Perhaps he did not want to face the changes time most certainly would have wrought to the places he and Sophia knew, instead wanting to preserve his beautiful memories. Or perhaps facing those places would be too painful without Sophia there on his arm.

And so, Grandfather would send me to Italy, alone. "For love," he said. Those two words encompassed so many things, I thought. He was sending me because he loved me. Because I loved Italy. Because he loved Italy. Because he had found love, great and true love, in Italy. And perhaps, because he hoped I might find love there as well.

I decided, however, that I did not want to spend only a week or two as a tourist. I wanted to experience Italy, the real Italy, as he had. I wanted to spend at least a year exploring Italy. But to be able to do that, I needed a job. After a little research, I discovered I could get a job teaching English as a second language. And so, after a little work, and prayers, and with some good luck thrown in, I found a position in Florence, the capital of Tuscany, and one of the most beautiful Renaissance cities in Italy, a city full of art, history, and culture. And of course, a city renowned for its excellent wine and food.

I was ecstatic. I was going to Tuscany!

And so, I finally arrived in Italy. I was based in Florence, in Tuscany, but I was able to travel to several other regions—from Sicily and Puglia in the south, to Veneto and Lombardia and the Trentino and Alto Adige in the north, and Abruzzo and Umbria to the east over the Apennines. And I fell in love with Italy all over again—with the wines, the food, the history, the towns, the wineries, the countryside, the people…everywhere I went, every town and trattoria, every vintner I met, every wine I drank, seemed to write a story for me.

I scribbled these stories in my little sketchbook, sometimes lazily as I sat in a field or at a table in a piazza, sometimes quickly before I fell asleep, and sometimes upon awakening the next morning, happily recalling the adventures of the previous evening. I was capturing the moment, to savor again and again over the years.

Sometimes, when I awoke in the morning, there was a story from a dream—about the wine, or the vineyard, or the day. Dreams such as these helped me remember many of the more subtle qualities of the previous day, which I might otherwise have overlooked in my recounting. Other dreams were more like time travel, taking me back into history, and seeming as real to me as yesterday.

And, there was Paolo.

When I returned home after my year in Italy, and had friends over to share dinner and a bottle of good Italian wine, I was asked time and again to tell some of those stories, my memories of Italy, the wineries and the wines. "Write them down for us," they asked, "so that we can sit by our fireside, or in the shade in the backyard, with a glass of good wine, and be back in Tuscany or Veneto with you."

And so, I have done just that, here in this book.

This is a book on wine, and it is my hope you'll learn a little more about some Italian wines in addition to the places, people, and practices followed in their creation. There will be some of the usual "wine geek" details, of course, but those will be related a little differently than you might expect. And because I love food and wine, you'll even find some recipes in the "food pairings" sections.

This is also something of a travel diary.

And it is also a storybook. Why? Well, because every bottle of wine has a story to tell.

Sometimes that story is a page out of a traveler's journal, sometimes a chapter out of a romance novel, sometimes a bit of history, sometimes something out of a dream. I know I'm not alone in feeling this way. José Andrés, the Spanish American chef often credited for bringing the "small plates" (tapas) dining concept to America, once said, "Every time I open a bottle of wine, it is an amazing trip somewhere." The English author D. H. Lawrence put it this way: "If we sip wine, we find dreams coming upon us out of the imminent night." I couldn't agree more.

For me, wine is as much of an experience as it is a flavor or taste. And so, for many wines, especially those I fell in love with, I can tell you where I was, who I was with, and all the details surrounding the situation. This book shares those experiences, as fully as it possibly could.

I've organized my wine stories by region, since this is a book on wine, rather than chronologically, as would better suit a travel diary or romance novel. I've included a map of Italy, below, for those less familiar with Italy's regions, or perhaps not sure exactly where in Italy a wine is from.

Each of Italy's twenty wine regions is unique, special, a new adventure, each as exciting and different as a new lover. And with so many different varieties of grapes (some 350 "authorized" varieties of grapes, although most Italians are quick to tell you there are really over 2,000 different varieties), it could take years to explore all these bottled treasures. "So many wines, so little time!"

If you can't find the specific boutique wines I've written about here on the shelves of your local purveyor of imported wines, and a trip to Italy is not in your immediate future, don't despair—look at the descriptions of the wine, consult with a wine-knowledgeable friend, or that helpful person in the wine store. I'm sure you'll find something that will be comparable to the wine I've described. Sample, and let each wine tell you its own unique story. I'm sure you'll find some worth "listening to" again!

Come. Join me now as we explore Italy. Together, let's experience the sights and sounds, the history and beauty, the outstanding cuisine, and most particularly, some terrific Italian wines.

Reader's Note: These stories are meant to be savored, like fine wine, or good food, or a wonderfully talented lover. Please don't overindulge or consume them too quickly. To get the most pleasure out of this book, I suggest you only read a few—one or two or three—at a time. Take your time with each one. Look into its depths, swirl, inhale, and sip slowly, using all your senses and imagination.

# Region: Tuscany/Toscana

**Wines:**

- Chianti
- Super Tuscan
- Tuscan Rosé
- Brunello
- Rosso di Montalcino

**Wineries:**

- La Moto
- L'Arco
- La Sala
- Ceppaiano
- Cava d'Onice

# Tuscany / Toscana

AH, TUSCANY—FOR ME, the essence of Italy, captured in the wine, the hilltop towns, the golds and greens of the fields, and the blue of the sky.

Tuscany, in central Italy, stretches from the Apennines to the Tyrrhenian Sea. Its capital, Florence, is home to some of the world's most recognizable Renaissance art and architecture, including Michelangelo's *David* statue, Botticelli's works in the Uffizi Gallery, and the Duomo basilica. Its diverse natural landscape encompasses the rugged Apennine Mountains, the island of Elba's beaches on the Tyrrhenian Sea, and the Chianti region's olive groves and vineyards.

No land is more caught up with the fruits of its fertile earth than Tuscany, the gourmet destination for foodies where locals too spend an inordinate amount of time thinking, talking, and consuming food and wine.

Come travel the backroads of Tuscany with me, and share my discoveries, dreams, and adventures.

## Chianti

Chianti is one of Italy's most well-known and recognized wines, tracing its history back to the thirteenth century, and taking its name from the Chianti region in the Italian province of Tuscany. The Chianti region is a large area of land stretching from the western reaches of the province of Pisa near the coast of the Tyrrhenian Sea, to Arezzo in the east, from the Siena hills to the south, to the Florentine hills in the province of Florence to the north.

Today's Chianti is *not* the Chianti my grandfather remembers from his time in Italy and what was available in the States for the next several decades after World War II. I'm also certain it is not the same Chianti my parents remember from their college days.

Gone is the Chianti that came in straw- or wicker-covered bottles, called fiaschi, which were often saved and used as candleholders. Back then, it was a fixture in inexpensive Italian restaurants, sinfully cheap and usually not very good—tart, acidic, and light-bodied. But, as I learned, the rules governing production of Chianti began to change in the late 1990s, significantly improving the quality of Chianti. Today, Chianti must be at least 80 percent Sangiovese grapes, and the other types of grapes which can be used, and percentages of each, are strictly specified. The high percentage of Sangiovese (translation: "the blood of Jove") gives Chianti its characteristic bright garnet color, cherry flavor, and aroma that makes one think of fresh violets. The bottles used have changed as well; most producers today have replaced the old straw-covered bottles with high-shouldered Bordeaux bottles.

Here are the stories told to me by five different bottles of Chianti, each a reflection of the winemaker, the vineyard, the grapes, and the moment.

# Memories of Tuscany—Inspired by La Moto Chianti

*Wine is a language that carries the culture of a country.*

—ROBERTO GULDENER

**STORY:** Drinking Chianti always takes me back to that wonderful year in Italy. My mind is flooded with memories—the little wine bars in Florence, such as Vinaino di Parte Guelfa, where they make the best sandwiches and friends wind up gathering outside on the street with a glass of Chianti in hand, or the wine bar Coquinarius, where I would enjoy the afternoon with a book, the ever-present Italian banter, and the pleasure of losing myself in a glass of wine.

And I remember the motorbike trips with Paolo through the Tuscan countryside, and sun-dappled piazzas in those little hill towns in Tuscany. One memory is particularly strong.

I am sitting outside a small trattoria. It may have been in Seggiano, or perhaps Volterra. The smell of roasting meat and a slow-cooking tomato sauce mingles with perfume of roses and the basil in the little herb garden as I sit, relaxed after a late lunch, sipping the house wine—a local Chianti. A young couple at the corner table share an intimate laugh, while a group at another table raise their glasses and celebrate the art of food that is the essence of Tuscan life with the toast "Buon Cibo, Buon Vino, Buoni Amici" ("Good Food, Good Wine, Good Friends"). I look at Paolo, daydreaming of sinful pleasures, and think for a moment that I could stay here forever. And in a way, when I open a bottle of Chianti, I am doing just that.

Chianti—a single word that floods my mind with the pleasures of every-day Italian life—a life characterized by a love for food and wine, a passion for life, and a love for family and friends. For Italians, time spent with family and friends is meant to be savored, with stories and reminiscences over good food and wine—often a good Chianti.

Tuscany is an enchanted land of rolling hills covered with fields of bright yellow sunflowers and red poppies glowing like fire in the sun, olive groves with their twisted branches and silvery leaves, and grapevines, hill towns, monuments, and art—it is the Italy of every foreigner's dreams. As you stand on a hill, the view of the silver of the olive trees, the green geometry of the vineyards, the roads lined with tall green cypresses, and the borders of the woods lined with yellow broom combine in a palette of colors that create a vibrant, inspiring, and wholly unique painting. The winding roads and cobblestone streets of the hill towns lend themselves to travel by small motorbikes (motorino) like the ubiquitous Vespa.

Wine has been a basic part of life here for centuries and as the simple fare has evolved, so has the wine. Perhaps in no other region of the world can one find wine estates that have produced wine for close to a thousand years. Not only do the Italians make wine, they also love to enjoy it.

Wine pervades the culture of Tuscany; it's a birthright. As one local winemaker said, "In Tuscany all we have is the land, the weather, the food, and the wine." And perhaps, you'd think, looking out over the land, "What else is there?" What else need there be? Because really, that's what life is all about (or should be). These things, and of course, friends and family to enjoy them with. As James Joyce, the Irish writer, so aptly put it, "What is better than to sit at the end of a day and drink wine with friends..."

**DESCRIPTION:** La Moto Chianti is a carefully crafted blend of three varieties of grapes from a number of select vineyards—80 percent Sangiovese, with the addition of 10 percent Canaiolo Nero and 10 percent Ciliegiolo grapes that bring a fruitiness that softens the tannins of the Sangiovese. A pleasant, easy-to-drink, traditional Chianti, it pairs well with most foods and is the perfect "everyday" wine. Meant to be enjoyed between three and five years after vintage, it has the potential to age for up to eight years.

**TASTING NOTES:** La Moto Chianti is medium-bodied, with the characteristic scent of violets on the nose, and the traditional Chianti flavors from the Sangiovese and Caniolo grapes, reminiscent of cherries.

**FOOD PAIRINGS:** Chianti is a wine built for everyday food. Of course, you can enjoy it with pasta with tomato-based sauces such as pappa al pomodoro, or pizza, or salami sandwiches, a Tuscan staple. It's also perfect with hearty soups such as a Tuscan bean soup, bread and cheese such as pecorino, and antipasto and bruschetta. It's also a good match for the many Italian chicken dishes featuring tomatoes.

# Mona Lisa Smile—Inspired by L'Arco Chianti

**STORY:** Paolo and I find Estate Arco on one of our motorbike ramblings into the Tuscan countryside one lovely weekend. It's a delightful small winery producing several wines under the L'Arco label, including a delightful Chianti. About twenty miles west of Florence, it is not far from the town of Vinci, birthplace of the first great artist of the Renaissance—Leonardo da Vinci. Perhaps in keeping with its association with Leonardo da Vinci, Estate Arco's winemaker tells us that here, to make wine is to make art. Art bottled and then enjoyed.

Perched in the mountains west of Firenze, Vinci may seem an unimposing little town, and yet it is full of the things that make a good life—grapes, olives, rosemary, and lavender. Vinci itself dates back to the early Middle Ages. In the town center we discover the Guidi castle, also known as the "castle of the ship" because of its elongated shape and the tower shaped like a sailing vessel. Guidi Castle is now home to the "Museo Leonardiano" (Leonardo Museum), which focuses on Leonardo's mechanical, scientific, and engineering inventions. The exhibits display Leonardo's work through models constructed according to the original dimensions drawn in his now famous "Notebooks."

We have lunch at "Il Ristoro Del Museo" not far from the museum, where we enjoy some of the best ribollita soup we've ever had, and a bottle of L'Arco Chianti. We raise a glass to the spirit of Leonardo, who we know from our reading also had a penchant for good food and good wine.

We hike up to visit Leonardo's boyhood home. It sits on a hilltop, at the end of a stony path winding up through olive trees. It's a quaint, ancient farmhouse, made of the golden and gray local stone. The view, however, is breathtaking—over the rolling hills, the leaves of the trees in the olive groves are shining silver in the sunlight. Vineyards glow in the distance, straight lines of green arching to the horizon. It's easy to imagine why his creativity would flourish here, being surrounded by such beauty at an early age.

Later that weekend, as we are sitting on the terrace of Estate Arco, enjoying the view and an impromptu picnic with another bottle of their Chianti, some local cheese, and a good loaf of bread, we have sense of déjà vu. "Where have we seen this view before?" I ask. "This is our first visit to the winery."

"Leonardo's house, perhaps?" Paolo questioningly replies.

"Yes, it is similar, but not quite the same. And come to think of it, that view from the hilltop also felt familiar."

Then, all of a sudden, I think I know why. I pull out a print I purchased in Vinci.

Let me share with you what I discovered in comparing that print to the view spreading out before me. Next time you look at Leonardo da Vinci's *Mona Lisa* (*La Gioconda*), don't focus on the half-smiling face, but notice instead the delicately painted landscape of hills, vineyards, castles, and cypress trees in the background. That's almost exactly the view you get as you look out from Leonardo's hilltop home, or the terrace of the Arco wine estate.

I hand the print to Paolo. He smiles, and agrees. There is now no reason to be surprised about the background landscape. Leonardo began the painting in 1503, in the town of Vignamaggio, home of the rich Gherardini family into which this lovely lady was born. Vignamaggio is just a few miles from Vinci, and this area was as well-known for its wineries at that time as it is today.

While no one knows for sure why the *Mona Lisa* is smiling that mysterious smile, I might venture a guess. I think perhaps she is thinking of the pleasures of sharing a glass or two of wine on a soft summer evening with her handsome and dashing husband, the rich silk merchant, Francesco del Giocondo.

**DESCRIPTION:** Wine has been produced here in Tuscany since the eighth century BC when the Etruscans made wine out the many grape varieties that grew here, including the Sangiovese.

L'Arco Chianti is artfully blended from Estate Arco vineyard grapes, using 90 percent Sangiovese and 10 percent of other varietals. The grapes are manually harvested, ensuring only the best are used to produce this lovely, full-bodied, and complex Chianti. From the Sangiovese grapes of Estate Arco comes the characteristic ruby-garnet color, cherry flavors, and a delightful spicy aroma. The other varietals blended with this high percentage of Sangiovese soften the wine, bringing a fruitiness and a subtle complexity.

This Chianti reflects the unique microclimate of this area and the skill of the L'Arco vintner. It is a smooth and satisfying wine, with deep flavor, a perfect everyday wine, though a cut above the average, pairing well with a wide range of foods. Wonderful three to six years after vintage, it has the potential to age well for several more years.

**TASTING NOTES:** L'Arco Chianti presents a depth and complexity of character and is more full-bodied than many other Chiantis. The first hints of this come as you bring the glass to your nose. Along with the traditional violet, cherry, and raspberry fragrances, you'll find it has spicy notes as well, and even hints of coffee. The taste follows—full, fruity, complex—artful and satisfying, a tribute to the winemaker as artist. It's an excellent example of today's Chianti wines, reflecting the Tuscan love of good simple food and good wine. If you enjoy a good wine with food, and don't want to have to think about which direction the vineyard was facing or the composition of the soil when you make a selection, this is the wine for you—just uncork, pour, and drink! Then take a quick look in the mirror—you, like the *Mona Lisa*, will be smiling. So will whoever is lucky enough to share a bottle with you.

**FOOD PAIRINGS:** Try this full-bodied Chianti with pasta with a meat ragù, red meats, or the quintessential soup of Tuscany—ribollita. Ribollita can take on many forms, from thin and broth-like, to thick like stew—a true comfort food. Its signature ingredients include day-old unsalted Tuscan bread, cavalo nero (black cabbage), white cannellini beans, kale, tomato, and often pancetta.

Or whip up a simple Tuscan bean salad—cannellini beans in olive oil with a generous amount of garlic, tomatoes, pepper, and herbs—parsley, thyme, basil. Let this "steep" for several hours to flavor the oil. Serve with Tuscan bread for dipping into that savory oil! Bring this as your contribution to a "potluck" dinner, along with a good Chianti and stand by for compliments.

For a wonderful and unique pairing, enjoy this with a tuna tartare—magnifico!

# The Legend of the Gallo Negro—Inspired by La Sala Chianti Classico

**STORY:** In the hills near San Casciano in Val di Pesa, about ten miles as the crow flies but somewhat longer on our motorbikes, we find La Sala Vineyards and Winery. The current owners are as knowledgeable about the history of their vineyard as they are about making wine. They take considerable pride in the fact that that the land was once owned by the famous de Medici family, from the fifteenth through the early eighteenth centuries.

Of course, wine has been made here since Roman times, and historical documents from the eleventh century speak of farmers selling their local wine to Florence wine merchants. The wine produced here was called "Chianti" after the name given to the area in the early Middle Ages, "Chianti Mountain." In honor of its history as the birthplace of Chianti, this small area of the Chianti region of Tuscany has been given the name "Classico," which is also applied to Chianti wine produced here today. Chianti Classico is generally acknowledged as the best of Tuscan Chiantis, and the La Sala Winery, as we discovered, produces a very nice Chianti Classico.

As the La Sala winemakers told me the history of the land and Chianti wine, and poured me a glass of their Chianti Classico, I wondered aloud, "Why is there a black rooster on a seal on the neck of the bottle?"

"Ah," they said, "that is the 'gallo negro'—the black rooster. It is the symbol and mark of a Chianti Classico, made to high standards, and of high quality. Why a black rooster, you may ask? Another bit of history and legend, going back almost eight hundred years to 1250."

I remember that afternoon, and the legend told, whenever I drink Chianti Classico.

*The Legend of the "Gallo Negro":*

*In the thirteenth century, the city-states of Florence and Siena were embroiled in what seemed to be an endless war over territory. First one would gain the upper hand, then the other. Various tactics were tried, including catapulting dead donkeys and dung over city walls in what* was the medieval equivalent of chemical and biological warfare. Needless to say, these battles were costly, unpopular, and disruptive. Finally, after some intensive negotiations, the cities agreed to settle their long-standing disputes over possession of land with a horse race.

The race would start at dawn, signified by the crowing of a rooster, with a knight leaving from his own city and racing toward the other city, some forty-four miles (seventy-one kilometers) away. The meeting point of the two knights would be the border of their territories. Each city chose its fastest horse and best rider. The choice of rooster was also important. Siena chose a white rooster and fed it well; the Florentines selected a black rooster and kept it for a few days in a box with no food. On the race day, the hungry Florentine rooster began crowing well before dawn, while the well-fed white rooster in Siena slept late. At the first crow, the knight of Florence swung up onto his horse and sped off at a gallop into the darkness, racing south toward Siena. He met the Sienese knight just twelve miles from the walls of Siena, in Fonterutoli, which left most of the Chianti territory united under Florentine rule. Since then, the black rooster has been the symbol of Chianti: first of the Chianti League in the fourteenth century and then of the Chianti Classico Consortium today.

And so, I thought, yes, to drink a Chianti Classico is to drink history—the history of Italian wine, and the history of this beautiful land—luscious, liquid history captured in each bottle.

**DESCRIPTION:** La Sala Chianti Classico is unique in that it is 100 percent Sangiovese, with no other varietals added. It exalts the elegant floral and bright cherry characteristics of Sangiovese, without adding the more common overtones of chocolate or coffee. As the La Sala winemaker explains, "We're traditional in the sense that we respect the traditions of the past, but we're not old-fashioned. We want a modern rendition of a time-honored wine that appeals to today's palates without betraying the tipicità of Sangiovese." We think you'll agree they've succeeded magnificently, once you taste this fine wine.

The Sangiovese grape is known for being extremely sensitive to external factors, such as terrain and climate, and it ripens late, and not at all uniformly. However, it is rare to find another variety that so faithfully interprets the characteristics of the soil in which it grows and modifies its odors in accordance with the terrain. *Sandstone* is responsible for the wine's flowery bouquet, *calcareous soils* produce scents of wild berries, and *tufa* or *volcanic* soils yield fresh odors of tobacco. But the scent of violets, a characteristic and specific element of Chianti Classico, is always present no matter where the vines grow.

La Sala hand-harvests their Sangiovese, selecting only the best, fully ripe grapes from each bunch. The result, after aging in oak for six months, and then six months in stainless steel, is a wine of unique and dazzling brilliance, with an earthy and floral charm.

**TASTING NOTES:** Chianti Classico are premium Chianti wines that tend to be medium-bodied with firm tannins and medium-high to high acidity. Floral, cherry, and light nutty notes are characteristic aromas, with the wines expressing more notes on the midpalate and finish than at the front of the mouth.

La Sala Chianti Classico is best oxygenated before serving, to release its full aromas and tastes. As you pour it into a tulip-shaped goblet, notice the deep ruby color and rich purple highlights. Bring it to your nose, and you'll recognize the trademark Sangiovese fragrance of violets, enhanced with complex fruity overtones of cherries and red currants. For a traditional "rustic" wine, the taste is surprisingly elegant and well-balanced, full of cherry and wild berry notes, and subtle spice and pepper. La Sala Chianti Classico is best served three years to six years after harvest.

**FOOD PAIRINGS:** A good Chianti Classico makes a fine accompaniment for all the many flavors of Tuscan cuisine, and you will naturally think of pairing it with red meats cooked on the grill, exemplified by the Tuscan classic "Bistecca alla Fiorentina." Rich and flavorful, and oh, so tender, this is a thick Porterhouse steak from Chianina beef, grilled over very hot coals, and always served rare.

Some of our other favorite food matches include grilled chicken, roast pork (aristo di maiale in Italy), pasta primavera, spicy vodka penne, and grilled eggplant. It's also excellent with earthy mushroom dishes, particularly those made with wild mushrooms, such as risotto ai funghi porcini. Just add a green salad, uncork the wine, and you have a true Tuscan dinner!

# Dining with the Three Ms—Inspired by La Sala Chianti Classico Riserva

**STORY:** Medici, Machiavelli, Michelangelo...these names roll over the tongue like a fine Chianti, great names in Italian history. Their histories are also the history of Tuscany, and of the Chianti Classico region in particular, where each of them lived for a time, and no doubt enjoyed the best wines the surrounding vineyards could offer. Both the Medici and the Machiavelli families owned vineyards here and produced wine; in fact, the La Sala vineyard, where Paolo and I are once again visiting, was owned by the Medici family.

It's a warm summer afternoon, with soft breezes moving through the vines where bees buzz lazily. We've splurged with a bottle of La Sala's Chianti Classico Riserva. We are soon lost in another world. Perhaps it is the wine, the warmth of the sun, the soft caresses of the Tuscan breeze, and the strong sense of tradition and history that permeates the vineyard, that combine to magically transport us back into another time.

There, just at the edge of my dream, a man is walking from the vineyard, wearing clothes in the style of centuries ago, dusty and sweaty from the day's labor. Who is that tall dark-eyed man, with the long aquiline nose? "Quite handsome," I think to myself, "and somehow familiar." Where have I seen him before? Perhaps in a commercial for a motorcycle, or for those aviator sunglasses that make anyone look sexy, especially Italian men?

And then I recognize him from my visit to the Uffizi Museum in Florence, the statue of Niccolò Machiavelli by Lorenzo Bertolini come to life. I seem to have drifted back to the early sixteenth century and found Niccolò on his family estate in San Casiano. Machievelli, credited today as the father of modern political science, wrote the classic manual for the ideal politician of the Renaissance, *The Prince*, here while exiled from Florence by the Medicis. But he did not just write—he also continued his father's work as an olive grower and winemaker, producing a wine called "Vermiglio." "Surely today," I muse, "he would be making this wine."

The scene shimmers and shifts. I'm now in a large room, hung with tapestries and lined with books, lit by the last amber rays of the sun and glowing, flickering candles. There is wine and food on the large, sturdy rustic table. I'm one of several guests, well-dressed gentlemen and ladies, joining Machievelli for dinner.

Wine is poured. We all raise our glasses in a toast to our host, and I take a sip. It's a wine suitable to the occasion, to the court of Machievelli. "Has this Chianti Classico Riserva also been transported back in time with me?" I wonder.

I suddenly recall reading a letter of Machievelli's describing this very scene: "When evening comes, I go back home, and go to my study. On the threshold, I take off my work clothes, covered in mud, and I put on the clothes an ambassador would wear. Decently dressed, I enter the ancient courts of rulers who have long since died. There, I am warmly welcomed, and I feed on the only foods I find nourishing and was born to savor. Four hours go by without my feeling any anxiety. I forget every worry."

My dream fades, and I am back in the present. Paolo and I talk over another glass of wine, and I discover that the magical time-travel dreams of the afternoon seem to have affected him as well. I describe my "visit" with Machievelli, which Paolo agrees may well have been inspired by the wine and influenced by our recent visit to the Uffizi and the research on Machievelli I did for one of my university courses. Then Paolo smiles and says, "Remember when I was researching Italian recipes from the Renaissance?"

"Yes." I smile.

That's one of the fascinating things about Paolo—sure, he's handsome and sexy, and he knows how to make me feel like a real woman, in that way that seems to come so easily and naturally to most Italian men, but he's also a great cook.

"And I found several recipes attributed to the court of Lorenzo di Medici?"

"Yes, of course, I remember," I say. "How could I forget? You created a fabulous dinner based on those recipes!"

"Then perhaps it's not surprising, being here on land once owned by the Medicis, who I think I just shared a glass of wine and dinner with in my dream."

I eagerly answer, "Lorenzo the Magnificent, probably the greatest single figure among the panoply of famous Medicis—poet, ruler, statesman, and Renaissance man. It has to be him. Lorenzo, whose life's works—his patronage of the arts, literature, learning, scholarship, and his own diverse poetry—earned him the title 'Il Magnifico.'"

Paolo's smile broadens further as he nods in agreement. "They were all there, the artists he knew and secured commissions for—Leonardo da Vinci, Ghirlandaio, Botticelli, and Michelangelo."

As Paolo describes the scene, I remember that Michelangelo is said to have lived with Lorenzo for five years, dining at the family table. I can only begin to imagine the conversations between Lorenzo and Michelangelo over glasses of the excellent wine from the Medici Estate. Perhaps if I drink another glass of this Chianti Classico Riserva, I can transport myself back to that time and place yet again. I wonder, will I be able to linger longer? Will the pasta be as good as Paolo's recreated recipe?

**DESCRIPTION:** The gold border on the seal with the black rooster (the "gallo negro") on the bottle of a Chianti Classico Riserva should tell you this is a special wine, and indeed it is. The best grapes are selected at the time of the harvest for the production of Riservas; only 20 percent of Chianti Classicos are good enough to wear the gold and the "Riserva" designation.

This La Sala Chianti Classico Riserva is made solely from hand-harvested Sangiovese grapes, carefully selected so only the very best grapes are used. Because it is 100 percent Sangiovese, it displays all the distinctive, unique, and enchanting characteristics of this grape to the fullest. The wine is aged for at least two years—a minimum of twelve months in oak, and then another six or more months in the bottle. While this wine can be enjoyed as soon as four years after harvest, it will reach its peak after a few more years in the cellar. The result is a wine that would not be out of place on the table of Lorenzo the Magnificent, or as a gift from Michelangelo to Pope Julius II—elegant, velvety, and with imposing structure.

**TASTING NOTES:** As with all great red wines, La Sala Chianti Classico Riserva is best oxygenated before serving, to release its full aromas and tastes. As you pour it into a large tulip-shaped goblet, enjoy the deep, rich ruby-red and garnet colors, almost glowing in the glass. In addition to the characteristic violet aroma of the Sangiovese grape, you'll sense lush ripe berries and complex spice tones—hints of cinnamon, pepper, and vanilla—as you swirl and bring it to your nose. The taste is magnificent—intense, with great depth and balance. Complex and fruity, with nuances of vanilla from its time in oak casks, tannins gentled by maturity. This is a truly elegant Chianti.

**FOOD PAIRINGS:** Chianti Classico Riserva is a wine for a special dinner, when you want the best. It is the ideal accompaniment for game dishes (venison, pheasant, lamb, or wild boar), or with aged cheeses. If you are splurging on a serious steak, grilled to rare perfection in the manner of the Tuscan specialty "Bistecca alla Fiorentina," go for the gusto and serve this wine. All you need add is a simple green salad.

Or, for something totally different, pair this with Lorenzo's Pasta, Paolo's re-creation based on his research on Renaissance and Medici court recipes. It's perfect for a memorable, history-based special dinner. The dish showcases ingredients that were all rare and costly in Lorenzo's day—oranges from Spain and spices from the East, served over pasta, with duck à l'orange, which was originally an Italian recipe. The pasta sauce is made from the juice of fresh-squeezed oranges and orange zest, simmered to reduce it until slightly thickened, seasoned with a hint of sugar and spices such as cinnamon and allspice. Paolo usually adds little duck or chicken stock, and a splash of a fruity white wine as well. Stir the sauce into al dente pasta, and slice the duck over top (we like boneless duck breast, pan seared and finished in a hot oven, skin crispy and meat tender and succulent). Garnish with peeled orange segments, sliced almonds, and a little fresh parsley or rosemary. Steamed green beans or fresh peas complement this nicely. Add candles and a bottle of Chianti Classico Riserva, and you might find yourself enjoying an idyllic evening in Lorenzo's court.

# Super Tuscan
# Revolutionary and Evolutionary

They are among the most enthralling and diversified wines in Italy, yet there is probably no term in Italian wine that is more slippery, vaporous, and misunderstood than "Super Tuscan."

Some people define Super Tuscan as a Tuscan blend made with Cabernet Sauvignon or other international varieties. Others define it as a wine that breaks ranks with Italy's strict Denominazione di Origine Controllata (DOC) quality regime. Others define it as any expensive wine from Tuscany.

The truth is Super Tuscan is all those things—and none of those things. While Sangiovese is the most common grape used in Super Tuscans and is most frequently combined with Cabernet Sauvignon, some Super Tuscans use Merlot or Cabernet Sauvignon exclusively and exclude Sangiovese altogether or use varying combinations of Merlot, Syrah, Cabernet Sauvignon, or other varieties. A Super Tuscan can be a 100 percent expression of Sangiovese with absolutely no international varieties. And the definition is changing all the time. To further complicate matters, since the blend can be practically anything, producers frequently fine-tune the wines by varying the composition of the blend from year to year.

To get a better grip on what these wines are, were, and will be it's best to start at the beginning—back in the Italy of the 1970s, when there was an enormous need to augment the rules governing Italian wine in order to achieve better quality and to become more competitive in foreign markets, specifically the United States. Super Tuscans (it's no coincidence the term is in English) proved to be the instrument with which both goals could be achieved.

In the 1970s, some Tuscan producers came to believe that the legal rules governing the production of Chianti were too restrictive. Some wanted to make wine outside of the allowed Chianti zone. They coined the term "Super Tuscan" to distinguish their wines from the inexpensive, low-quality wines that were associated with the term *vino da tavola*, or "table wine," that they were being forced to put on the label by the existing regulations.

Today, most Super Tuscans use the legal appellation of IGT (Indicazione Geografica Tipica), which gives producers more flexibility than Chianti and other Tuscan DOCs and more prestige than *vino da tavola*. The wines tend to be modern, big, and rich—and often carry a price tag of $100 or more a bottle.

Some Super Tuscans do contain Sangiovese, either 100 percent or in blends. But others are made solely from Merlot (such as the famous Tenuta dell'Ornellaia Toscana Masseto), from a blend of Cabernet Sauvignon and Syrah (Riccardo Baracchi Toscana Ardito), or from even more unusual blends, like an amalgamation of Petit Verdot, Cabernet Sauvignon, Syrah, and Merlot (Argiano Toscana Solengo).

Chianti's old traditional recipe called for a large proportion (between 10 percent and 30 percent) of white grapes to produce a diluted, fruity blend that could be consumed young and had virtually no shelf life. This is what Italy had to offer foreign markets at the same time that the rest of the world was enjoying its love affair with the sophisticated wines of Bordeaux.

In 1970, Marchese Piero Antinori, head of one of the most prestigious and oldest wineries in Tuscany, decided it was time to throw the book at the DOC. He introduced the vineyard-designate Tignanello, which contained Cabernet Sauvignon and Cabernet Franc and was aged in French oak barrels. The first vintage, 1971, was released in 1974. Though it was given a *Vino da Tavola* (table wine) designation by the DOC, it was not priced like an inexpensive table wine, but rather like a very good French Bordeaux. Piero's innovations and efforts at improving the quality of Italian wines to compete on the world stage have been recognized with numerous awards, including the "Leonardo Prize for Italian Quality" in 2004.

What Antinori had accomplished was truly revolutionary. Tignanello opened the floodgates to international grape varieties like Cabernet Sauvignon, Cabernet Franc, Petit Verdot, Merlot, Syrah, and others that were not eligible for Tuscany's various appellations.

Antinori's uncle, Marchesi Incisa della Rocchetta, had already been making a small production of the Bordeaux-inspired Sassicaia since 1968 in

Bolgheri, and together these two wines sparked a wine renaissance worthy of Michelangelo and Leonardo da Vinci's birthplace.

Today, almost every Tuscan estate produces at least one Super Tuscan, and there is a formidable parade of Super Tuscans with enigmatic names on wine-shop shelves. While producers have great flexibility in the names they give to their Super Tuscan wines, it is a rare Tuscan estate that doesn't name its wine after some ancestor or family member, some personal whimsy, or some geographic feature of the estate or vineyard.

Yes, it's true that most Super Tuscans tend to carry very expensive price tags. Fortunately for those of us not comfortable with mortgaging our financial future in order to purchase a few "cult" or other superpopular Super Tuscans, there are some reasonably priced Super-Tuscans available that generally don't get a lot of play in the popular press and consequently offer good value for the dollar. These are the ones I sought out in Tuscany.

# Bacchus Comes to the Book Club — Inspired by La Moto Toscano Sangiovese Super Tuscan

**STORY:** I remember my first time. Doesn't everyone? It was that dashingly handsome Giotto who introduced me to it.

Before you get the wrong idea, I mean my "first time" savoring a glass of Super Tuscan wine. It was before I went to Italy, and it made me all the more eager to go and explore the wines of Tuscany, up close and personal.

My friend Giotto arrives, as usual, on his motorbike. He's brought the wine to our "Finer Things Book Club" meeting today. I don't remember the book we were reviewing, except that it was set in Tuscany. But I do remember the food and the wine—definitely "Finer Things."

In keeping with our club tradition, our food and wine for the evening reflect the book we are reading and discussing. And so Giotto has conspired with Lisa, our hostess, to transport us to his home in Tuscany. Lisa's kitchen table is full of antipasto—salami, prosciutto and melon, prosciutto and asparagus, several kinds of cheese, roasted peppers, kalamata olives, focaccia, and bruschetta.

"I don't know what I would have done without Giotto," whispers Lisa. "He found real Italian salami, prosciutto, and cheeses, and gave me the recipes for the focaccia and authentic bruschetta. He spent half the afternoon here helping, before he went out to get the wine."

That's Giotto—he always seems to bring the spirit of that magical region with him wherever he goes.

The wine is from Tuscany, of course. Giotto jokes that he only bought it because of the "La Moto" on the label, but we trust his taste in wine and know he's brought an Italian gem for us to enjoy.

Later, after our discussion, Giotto shares a little more about his homeland with us. He explains that this wine, La Moto Toscano, is a "Super Tuscan." It's a wonderfully drinkable blend of Sangiovese, the traditional grape of Tuscany, and Cabernet Sauvignon, a much more recent addition to the Italian vineyards. Piero Antorini—a relative, Giotto assures us—created the first "Super Tuscan" back in the early 1970s by blending Cabernet Sauvignon with

Sangiovese. He wanted to make a better red wine, "a wine to match the best from France," he vowed. His wine would be different from the Chianti of those days, combining the best of Italian wine-making tradition with a more modern style, and aged in French oak as are most premium wines today. We toast "Prozio Piero" (Great-Uncle Piero) and agree he certainly succeeded, as evidenced by the La Moto Toscano we are enjoying.

Later that evening, Giotto entertains us by reciting verses from a very old Italian poem, "Bacco in Tuscana."

*Like a king*
*In his conquering*
*Chianti wine with his red flag goes,*
*Down to my heart, and down to my toes;*
*He makes no noise, he beats no drums,*
*But pain and trouble fly when he comes.*

He explains this was written in 1685 by Francesco Redi to celebrate the wine of Tuscany. It is a sort of hymn to the god of wine, and recounts the arrival of Bacchus in Tuscany, along with Ariadne and a host of satyrs, nymphs, and Baccantes. The poem describes how the entire party partakes liberally of Tuscan wine, with much singing and wild dancing, and that all praise the wonderful wine of Tuscany. While our gathering is somewhat more refined and restrained, we too raise our glasses and toast Giotto and this delightful "Super Tuscan" wine.

**DESCRIPTION:** Italian reds speak a language all their own—a language of the marriage of good food, good wine, and good friends. Italian red wines have never been better, and the Super Tuscans with their distinctive personalities are appealing more and more to wine lovers across the world. La Moto Toscano is a great example, a blend of 85 percent Sangiovese and 15 percent Cabernet Sauvignon. It reflects the personality and taste of the vintner, who wanted to create a premium international-style wine that would appeal to the modern palate, yet retain its Tuscan soul—a wine meant to be enjoyed with good food. This is a very easy-to-drink wine, not too structured, aged twelve months in small French barriques, suitable for almost any occasion. Like any premium red wine, La Moto Toscano should be opened and oxygenated before drinking. It can be enjoyed six to eight years after vintage and has good potential for aging.

**TASTING NOTES:** I swirl the ruby-red La Moto Toscano in my glass and note the scent of violets, from the Sangiovese grapes, with hints of strawberries and pepper from the Cabernet Sauvignon. It is a soft, harmonious red wine, tasting of black cherries and dark chocolate, a wonderful example of a Super Tuscan wine.

**FOOD PAIRINGS:** This versatile and delicious Toscana Super Tuscan can be enjoyed with a multiplicity of dishes. Of course, it's perfect with traditional Italian and Tuscan fare such as robust antipastos, hearty soups like ribolitto, pastas, and pizza. It complements hearty meals of grilled meats and even roasted chicken. Take this along to any social gathering where you want to make a great impression with your taste in wine.

# In the Footsteps of Galileo — Inspired by Ceppaiano Super Tuscan / Toscano

**STORY:** Inspired by a recent celebration of Galileo Galilei's 450th birthday, Paolo and I are winding our way along the Arno River to his birthplace in Pisa. Paolo's motorbike hugs the curves, and I hug Paolo. The wind ruffles our hair. The Arno meanders through the heart of Tuscany, from Florence to Pisa and then into the Mediterranean Sea. The river valley and the surrounding rolling hills are not only beautiful; they hold innumerable vineyards that have produced wine for thousands of years. Paolo and I decide to stop at one of them, Ceppaiano, and soon fall in love with their Toscano Super Tuscan.

We reflect on Galileo as we sip our wine. Living in this land, where good food and good wine are a way of life, we were not surprised to learn that the Galelei family had a vineyard and that Galileo appreciated good wine.

When Galileo was just a boy of ten, his family moved to Florence, where his father became a Medici court musician. Galileo grew up in that beautiful city, as renowned then as it is today for its wine and its food, as well as its art. Galileo must have loved the city as much as we do, because throughout his life, he would remain close to the Medici court and Tuscany, visiting often, even after moving to Padua, in northeast Italy, to teach mathematics at the university there.

Galileo, with his brilliant, restless, and inquisitive mind, and perhaps because of his association with the Medici family, had contact with many of the great scientists and intellects of his day, across Italy as well as Europe, including those surrounding the pope. We can envision Galileo and the pope's physician, Andrea Bacci, who was also a botanist, discussing the wines of Tuscany. Perhaps that inspired Bacci to tour Tuscany and write, in 1596, *De Naturali Vinorum Historia* (*The Natural History of Wines*), in which he described Tuscan wines as "exquisite, generous and ruby-red elixers"—a description Bacci would no doubt have applied to Super Tuscan wines.

In 1608, Galileo returned to Florence, invited to attend the wedding of Cosimo de Medici. One can only imagine the lavish feasting and the wines served at the wedding banquet. Perhaps Galileo took the opportunity to express to Cosimo his longing to return to his beloved Tuscany? Two years later, Cosimo, now the grand duke of Tuscany, appointed Galileo "Chief Mathematician of the University of Pisa" and "Philosopher and Mathematician to the Grand Duke of Tuscany." And so Galileo returned home, to Florence, and published his book, *The Starry Messenger*, that described the many incredible observations he had made of the stars and planets in our solar system, through the eyepiece of the telescope he had fashioned with his own hands. Six years later, after publishing letters supporting the heliocentric view of the universe and falling out of favor with the Vatican, he retired to his family estate just outside Florence and lived amid the vineyards he loved.

I believe Galileo would have appreciated "Super Tuscan" wines and the winemakers of the 1970s who sought to make an international premium-style wine that defied the strict regulations that controlled the "formula" for Chianti wine. Since Galileo defied the strictures of the Catholic Church when he supported the theory of Copernicus that the sun was the center of the solar system, he would have no doubt felt these vintners to be kindred spirits.

How appropriate, then, to raise a glass of Ceppaiano Toscano Super Tuscan wine to toast Galileo on his birthday, February 15, or those bold Tuscan winemakers who gave us "Super Tuscans," with a quote from Galileo himself: "Wine is sunlight, held together by water."

**DESCRIPTION:** This is an exceptional example of a Super Tuscan wine, having been awarded 90 points by *Wine Spectator*. Located on the edges of the Arno River about twenty-five kilometers from the Tyrrhenian Sea, the Ceppaiano Estate vineyard has been producing quality wines since 1903. The sandy soil, rich in minerals and fossils of marine origin, contributes great flavor and character to the grapes, and thus to the wine. The proximity of the Mediterranean, long summers, marine breezes, and the light soils of the coast result in wines with great complexity and concentration.

The use of integrated organic cultivation techniques, hand-picking of the grapes, and immediate fermentation in the vinification cellar inside the vineyard allows the preservation of the pureness of the fruit from cultivation to harvest and transformation into Ceppaiano Toscano Super Tuscan. It is aged for twelve months in French oak barrels, in the manner of modern, international-style, premium red wines, and then additionally aged for several years before release.

The result of all this care is a wonderful "Bordeaux-blend" Super Tuscan in the Brunello style, 90 percent Sangiovese, 10 percent Cabernet Sauvignon.

Ceppaiano Toscano Super Tuscan is ready to be enjoyed about six years after vintage, and it should age well for several more years. As with all super-premium, aged red wines, this wine should be opened and oxygenated for a minimum of one hour before serving.

**TASTING NOTES:** Open a bottle of Ceppaiano Toscano Super Tuscan, and pour it into a glass decanter for oxygenation before serving. Give it a minimum of an hour, perhaps more, to develop its full bouquet and taste. You'll notice the beautiful, intense, and dark ruby-red color. As you pour it into your glass and swirl, you'll appreciate the complex and intriguing aromas, so much more than the usual scent of violets and cherries typical of Sangiovese-based wines. Yes, those are there, but like a good perfume with layers of scents, you'll also detect wild roses growing by the sea, mint, black currants, and licorice, followed by hints of oak and sweet coffee.

And the taste—complex and intriguing. Run it over your tongue and savor it. There is a lovely combination of plum and spice, complemented by chocolate, vanilla, and buttery oak, with a long finish.

**FOOD PAIRINGS:** Ceppaiano Toscano Super Tuscan complements almost all Italian cuisine, of course, from pasta to that wonderful Italian version of grilled steak, Bistecca alla Fiorentina. Pair this with a hearty lasagna, complemented by a Tuscan bread salad and roasted vegetables for a satisfying meal on a winter's evening. Or try it with spicy Mediterranean dishes from its birthplace near the sea, perhaps some thick, juicy, Mediterranean-spiced grilled lamb chops, teamed with roasted potatoes or polenta with roasted Mediterranean vegetables (eggplant, zucchini, onions, peppers, garlic, and some sun-dried tomatoes), and spinach sautéed with garlic, and you'll have an elegant dinner, fit for a Medici.

# A Tuscan Queen Transforms France—Inspired by La Sala Campo All' Albero Toscano

**STORY:** My good friends Jon and Jean are returning from a month housesitting in France, a wonderfully affordable way to have an extended honeymoon. They stop by Florence for a visit before heading home to the States. To celebrate their wedding and time in France, we are on the trail of a Bordeaux-style Tuscan wine and find ourselves at the La Sala winery, one of my favorites.

The wine that Francesco, the owner, opens for us for the occasion is La Sala Campo All'Albero ("A tree in the field") Toscano, a Bordeaux-style blend of Cabernet Sauvignon and Merlot. The wine takes its name from the lone tree that stands in the Cabernet Sauvignon vineyard. The picnic spot Francesco has recommended for us overlooks that vineyard and the huge, ancient tree in its center. He says that estate "legend" has it that the tree is several hundred years old, and several Italian poets and authors occasionally have made their way to this field and found inspiration for their work as they sat in the shade of this magnificent tree enjoying bread, cheese, and wine. He looks at me and winks. "Perhaps you will find inspiration here as well.

"I also imagine," he says, "that members of the Medici family, who once owned this land, may have also enjoyed this very tree when they visited the estate to escape the heat of Florence. Or," he says, pausing to consider another possibility, "perhaps they planted it and watched it grow apace with their vineyards.

"Of course," he points out, "the Cabernet Sauvignon vines are a much more recent addition. We planted those. This field is perfect for them, but we couldn't bring ourselves to cut down that magnificent tree to make room for more vines. It reminds us too much of the history of this land."

Picnic and recommended wine in hand, we are soon comfortably situated for an afternoon of good food, good conversation, and good wine. Paolo and I are eager to hear about Jon and Jean's adventures.

"Of course it was wonderful," Jean says. "We visited some of the most beautiful chateaus. I think my favorite was Chateau de Chenonceau, in the Loire Valley. I liked it even better than Fontainebleau.

"I learned that Chenonceau was Caterina de Medici's favorite residence as well. Remember, she was the niece of Lorenzo the Magnificent, who, in 1533, at the tender age of fourteen, married Henry of Orleans, the second son of the king of France. In 1547, Henry became king of France, and Caterina, queen," Jean continues. "I wonder if she visited this Medici estate before she left for France?"

Jean has a real penchant for history. She reads history voraciously, especially histories of significant women, the way some other women read romance novels.

"Maybe," I wonder to myself, thinking of Francesco's remark about this location, "she will be inspired to make historical documentaries?"

Jean continues, "Henry's death in 1559 thrust Caterina into the political arena. She served as advisor to the frail oldest son, Francis II. When he died just a year later, Caterina became regent on behalf of her ten-year-old son, Charles IX, and had broad powers over the court and France. When her third son, Henry III, ascended the throne in 1574, Caterina continued to play a key role in governing France, until her death in 1589. She was the most powerful woman in sixteenth-century Europe, and changed the face of France in many ways, not all of which were political.

"You see, when Caterina arrived in France, she was most likely shocked by the relatively rustic and rather primitive trappings (by her standards) of the French court compared to the Italian court she was used to—French food served at court had no fancy sauces, offering only simple roast meats. Caterina brought with her to France the elegance of the Florentine and Papal courts, and a love of fine dining, including of course the best wines. Did you know she was orphaned at a young age and raised by Cardinal Guilo de Medici, who became pope?

"She brought luxurious table settings and introduced the use of the dinner fork. She also brought her own cooks, who introduced the secrets and refinement of Italian cooking to France, including peas, beans, artichokes, duck in orange *(canard à l'orange)*, onion soup *(carabaccia)*, sorbets and ice creams, marmalades, fruits in syrup, pastry making, and of course, pasta. This new style of cooking and dining profoundly influenced French cuisine over the next centuries."

"Oh, Jean," I say, "that sounds like a story with all the makings of great historical documentary."

"Yes," agrees Paolo, who is our resident foodie, "a Tuscan queen reforms the medieval French cooking tradition, so it is reborn as the modern French cooking we know today."

We raise our glasses in a toast to inspiration and to Caterina, presiding over an elegant table, set with fine silverware and crystal goblets, enjoying the refined and elegant cuisine she introduced to the French royal court, with a wine like this La Sala Campo All'Albero Toscano.

**DESCRIPTION:** La Sala Campo All'Albero Super Tuscan is an excellent example of a "Bordeux-blend" Tuscan red. The winemaker at La Sala originally made this wine with a very high percentage of Cabernet Sauvignon (85 percent) and a lower percentage of Sangiovese (15 percent). More recently, the blend has shifted to 50 percent Cabernet Sauvignon and 50 percent Merlot. This, and longer aging, has resulted in a richer, more complex wine.

The grapes are all hand-harvested and carefully selected. Like all Super Tuscans, this is made in a more modern and international style than traditional Chiantis, aging for about eighteen months in barrels made from fine-grained slightly roasted French oak, then at least twelve months in the bottle. While Campo All'Albero is clearly a modern premium red, it is Italian in its soul, better on the dinner table than sipped alone, with a strong backbone of acidity that is best enjoyed with food.

True to its heritage as a superpremium red, La Sala Campo All'Albero has a lot of aging potential and won't reach maturity for about eight years after vintage. This is definitely a wine to be aged for at least six years after vintage. When you do open a bottle, be sure to give it plenty of time for oxygenation to mellow and release its full aromas and flavors, at least an hour, preferably longer.

**TASTING NOTES:** La Sala Campo All'Albero is a deep, intense, and bright ruby red. Please serve at about sixty-five to sixty-eight degrees Fahrenheit, after oxygenating for at least an hour. The bouquet is intense with fruit, spice, and balsamic notes. The flavor mirrors the nose, with dark fruits and spice. It is rich, warm, and robust, with a silky or almost velvety texture, thanks to the soft tannins. This is a gorgeous example of a Super Tuscan, and truly a wine fit for a royal court.

**FOOD PAIRINGS:** Elegant and robust, this wine complements all red meats, as well as game of all kinds, as you would expect of a Cabernet Sauvignon and Merlot blend. We love it with a Florentine beef stew, venison, boar or pork, and even with pheasant and duck.

For a meal reminiscent of the court of Henry II and Caterina de Medici, try this La Sala Campo All'Albero with robust onion soup and duck à l'orange or fine chateaubriand.

# The Ghost of Leonardo—Inspired by L'Arco Noir

*All great acts of genius began with the same consideration: do
not be constrained by your present reality.*

—Leonardo da Vinci

**STORY:** Do you ever buy a bottle of wine just because of the artistry of the label, the shape of the bottle, or the name? I know I do, but then I like to experiment. Sometimes I'm disappointed, but many times I discover a wonderful wine.

Many Super Tuscans carry unique names, and I often wonder about the inspiration for, or meaning of, the name. If I visit the winery, I often ask about the name. Sometimes the explanation is perfectly logical, like La Sala Campo All'Albero ("A tree in the field"), which takes its name from an old tree that grows in the center of the La Sala Cabernet Sauvignon vineyard, the source of the grapes for the wine.

Sometimes we find ourselves at home with a bottle of wine with an intriguing name, no one to ask about it, and no obvious reason or meaning behind the name. Then, Paolo and I will play a game and try to "reverse engineer" the story behind the name of the wine. The rules are that there must be some logic behind the story, the story must relate to the name of the wine, it must be creative, and we must finish the story by the time we have finished the bottle of wine.

And so, one rainy evening, we are enjoying a bottle of L'Arco Noir. It's an unusual very dark red wine from Tuscany, a blend of Merlot, Syrah, and Sangiovese, known as a Bordeaux-blend-style "Super Tuscan" wine. L'Arco Noir comes from the Estate Arco winery in the hills of northern Tuscany, near Vinci, the birthplace of Leonardo da Vinci. These facts are known to Paolo and me, and they mark the starting point for our challenge.

And so the game begins: "What's in a name?" we think to ourselves.

Well, we know "Noir" is a French word. That means we have a French name, for an Italian wine. This should be interesting!

"Noir"—that means black or dark in French. So that fits.

And Merlot is the French name for a young blackbird—another connection.

And then there's the vineyard connection with Leonardo da Vinci, the archetype of the Renaissance man—artist, musician, mathematician, scientist, engineer, inventor, philosopher. And vineyard owner.

How is that related to the name "Noir," you might ask?

Well, Leonardo spent the last years of his life not in his beloved Italy, but in west-central France at the court of King Francis I, at Chateau d'Amboise. He is even buried in the Chapel of Saint-Hubert in Chateau d'Amboise.

What kinds of wines might have graced the royal table there in Chateau d'Amboise? Since we can trace Merlot back to the first century in France and Syrah to the third century, perhaps wines made from those grapes were enjoyed by Leonardo. And perhaps he brought some of the best Tuscan Sangiovese wine, also a favorite of the pope, with him to share with the king of France.

We know Leonardo appreciated good wine, because he wrote, "The discovery of a good wine is increasingly better for mankind than the discovery of a new star." We might imagine Leonardo, wine lover and vineyard owner, scientist and inventor, thinking how these grapes might grow in his own vineyard in Italy, and what kinds of wines he might have made from them, blended in different ways.

I think we're onto something here with these connections.

Today, the vineyards in the Tuscan hills not only grow Sangiovese grapes, as they have for thousands of years, but since the 1800s, French imports such as Merlot, Syrah, and Cabernet Sauvignon have been planted in Italian vineyards as well. And, for the past forty years, some of Tuscany's best vintners have been experimenting with blending these varietals to create a premium red wine for the modern palate, yet based on the traditions of the best of Italian wine making. The result is a class of wines known simply, and perhaps appropriately, as "Super Tuscan" wines. Stylish and sophisticated, they stand on a par with the best premium wines in the world. So, just as Leonardo da Vinci's works changed people's perception of painting, sculpture, mechanics, and science, these Super Tuscans changed people's perceptions of Italian wine.

We continue with our musings.

What if the spirit of Leonardo, vineyard owner, wine lover, artist, and inventor, returned to the hills of Tuscany one dark night, not so long ago? And if it did, did his spirit whisper suggestions into the dreams of vintners seeking to make a premium wine, in the international style, free from the restrictions imposed on the making of the more familiar Chianti?

Did Leonardo's spirit infuse their dreams with ideas of using a wider palette of grapes, of experimenting with blending wine from French grapes now grown in Italy with the traditional Sangiovese wine? Did his spirit encourage those vintners to "not be constrained by (their) present reality"?

Is the name "Noir" a nod to this mysterious source of inspiration, along with the deep, dark color of this wine?

We may never know, but we can imagine Leonardo would be proud of this blend of soft, fruity Merlot, full-bodied Syrah, and classic Sangiovese.

With our last glass of "Noir," we toast with Leonardo's own words, "All great acts of genius began with the same consideration: do not be constrained by your present reality."

**DESCRIPTION:** L'Arco Noir is an innovative "Bordeaux-blend" style Super Tuscan wine, 40 percent Merlot, 40 percent Syrah, and 20 percent Sangiovese. This wine is aged in oak for about fourteen months, with additional bottle aging for at least six months. The result is a wine of depth and complexity, excellent with food, smooth and satisfying. L'Arco Noir is a stellar example of modern Italian wine making, blending tradition with innovation to create a great red wine. And, unlike many Super Tuscans, it is affordable for the average red-wine lover.

To enjoy this wine to its fullest, we suggest decanting and allowing the wine to open with oxygenation for about two hours before serving.

**TASTING NOTES:** Ah, L'Arco Noir…as you pour it, admire its intense, deep ruby-red color—dark, inviting, mysterious. Decanted and oxygenated, the bouquet is complex and intriguing as you swirl and bring it to your nose—take a moment or two to appreciate all the layers and elements—dark fruits and cherries, with delicate hints of mint, licorice, and pepper, and even sweet cocoa. And then the taste…smooth and complex, with soft tannins, rich flavors of dark cherries and dark chocolate, nuances of oak. A delightful wine that combines the elegance and suppleness of Merlot and Syrah with the austerity of Sangiovese. Balanced and approachable in its youth with considerable aging potential (five to eight years), this is a wine to enjoy again and again.

**FOOD PAIRINGS:** Be as innovative as Leonardo da Vinci and the Italian winemakers who created these Super Tuscan wines. This Super Tuscan not only enhances Sunday dinners and special occasions, but, with its great value, will lend élan and panache to those Monday leftovers.

Of course, it's also wonderful paired with grilled meats, steaks and roasts, or game such as venison, and roasted vegetables, but do try it with grilled salmon, mushroom-based dishes (especially those made with porcini mushrooms), or the Sicilian dish arancini (balls of rice that are stuffed and deep-fried)—try making it with smoky gouda cheese and beef chorizo sausage stuffing for something delightfully different. Good accompaniments include rapini, chard, and kale, as well as polenta or white beans. And perhaps dark-chocolate-dipped strawberries for dessert?

# Why We All Want to Go to Italy—Inspired by L'Arco Syrah Dolce Vita

*In Tuscany, the "sweet life" (la dolce vita) involves friends and family sharing good food and good wine, "the poetry of the earth."*

**STORY:** From childhood, I always wanted to go to Italy. So let me ask you— "If money were no object, which country outside the United States would you choose for a vacation?" Would you be surprised to learn that Italy has placed either first or second as the top vacation choice for Americans, according to Harris Polls conducted for the past eight years? I wasn't, but that bit of information did get me thinking, over a glass of wine, of course, about the reasons why. I even "polled" some of my American friends. The answers all seemed to revolve around that most Italian concept, "*la dolce vita.*"

Italy promises to provide an experience so different from our busy American daily lives. There is the long history of Italy, visible everywhere, which seems to put time in perspective—don't rush; you have all the time in the world to accomplish or experience something. And then there are all the Italian traditions, based around family, friends, food, and wine. And of course, the Italian philosophy and way of life—the art of taking one day at a time and enjoying every minute is such a contrast to the hustle and bustle of American life, racing past the roses. In Italy, there seems to be a relaxed attitude toward making the best of what one has, and of taking pleasure in all that life provides, in living with simplicity and joy. Taking time for a good glass of wine and a good meal, home-cooked or in a good restaurant, and shared with those you care about, whether family or friends, seems guaranteed to reduce stress and increase the pleasures of life. Who doesn't want to savor that?

And romance, of course—the romance that Italy seems so known for— another aspect of *la dolce vita.* The very thought of Italy can inspire visions of passion and romance in the most stoic of hearts. There are lovers, young and old, around every corner, it seems. And perhaps a lover waiting to be discovered, as you wander through the soft, sensual Italian day or night. The dark-eyed young men and women, who seem to exude sensuality from every pore. Who knows where you might find the love of your life, or a secret sweet liaison? In a trattoria, in a wine bar, in a museum, on a hiking trail? And if you don't post to Instagram or Facebook, what happens in Italy could stay in Italy, and of course safely in your memories.

And then there is the sheer beauty of Italy—Renaissance-painting landscapes, castles, monasteries, and churches standing sun drenched, flowered, and frescoed. Beautiful stone villas perched on cliffs over glistening seas. Charming outdoor cafés inviting you to while away a lazy afternoon; soft, sweet music flowing through the streets like a part of the very air you breathe. Lively piazzas where children's laughter echoes through the streets. Starry nights that beckon lovers to stroll down cobblestone alleyways rich with antiquity.

And food, one of the cornerstones of Italian culture. From that initial crescendo of antipasto to a last indulgent bite of tiramisu, every authentic Italian dish is built on the most basic yet most flavorful ingredients based on seasonality and locality. It's rich and textural and uses a full palette of flavors, meant to be lingered over and savored. It evokes images of a mother or grandmother or wife or lover, for whom cooking is truly an expression of love. It has been said that Italian food comes from, and expresses, the emotions of the person cooking, that it is food designed to be simply enjoyed and experienced, not studied intellectually. Consider, for example, the joys of fried squash blossoms, sitting fat, stuffed with wine-soaked mushrooms, or gelato in any one of one hundred flavors, cool and soft and voluptuous on your tongue (in Rome, try St. Crispin's, around the corner from the Trevi Fountain—I'll confess to having two scoops one hot afternoon and deciding I just had to go back for two more, it was so good). Walk through the markets bursting with a rainbow of produce, cheeses, meats, seafood, and flowers, and alive with the songs of the day's fishermen.

And of course, the wine…such an important part of Italian life and *la dolce vita*. I, like the winemakers at L'Arco, have to agree with the famous Italian philosopher, writer, and poet Mario Soldati, who wrote: "Wine is the poetry of the earth."

Yes, Italy is a bounty, a feast for all senses, romance come to life for those of us brought up among concrete modernity and fast-food burgers.

I'm truly living *la dolce vita* here in Florence and about to share it with some friends, arriving soon for dinner. Would you like to join us? I'll put on some music, and the bottle of L'Arco Dolce Vita Syrah I'm opening will provide the poetry.

**DESCRIPTION:** Is this a "Super Tuscan" or not? Some say yes; some say no, the definition of "Super Tuscan" being rather, ahem, fluid. I don't want to argue about what classification this falls under, but it is from Tuscany. It's made with an "international" grape, Syrah, and it's pretty darn good.

L'Arco Dolce Vita Syrah (Shiraz to you Aussie fans) is a lovely example of an Italian Syrah, lightly oaked to provide complexity, structure, and elegance, without detracting from the fresh, fruity, spicy flavors this grape is known for.

Native to the Rhone valley in southern France, Syrah has been grown in Italy, from Sicily to Tuscany, since the 1800s. This grape has set up iconic strongholds in Australia and California, but it is only beginning to show what it is capable of doing when combined with Italian terroir and wine-making art. Estate Arco's vineyards are near Vinci, where the climate and terroir are well suited to Syrah. And L'Arco's vintner is producing wonderful "bottled poetry" from these grapes.

L'Arco selectively hand-picks the grapes for this wine. They are softly de-stemmed and crushed , and the juice flows by gravity into stainless-steel tanks, where it ferments  for ten days at a controlled temperature. Maceration on the skins continues for an additional three weeks. The wine is then racked into new oak tonneaux, and remains there for some nine months before bottling.

The winemaker recommends serving at about sixty to sixty-five degrees Fahrenheit and, as with all good red wines, opening and allowing the wine to breathe and oxygenate to allow all the luscious flavors to develop.

**TASTING NOTES:** L'Arco Dolce Vita Syrah is distinguished by its intense ruby-red color with shades of purple, clear and bright. The nose opens elegantly, with aromas of red fruits like plum, blackberry, and cherry, with hints of mocha. This is a big, intense, and full-bodied wine, yet complex and subtle. Though oak-aged, it retains a fresh and fruity taste; it is smooth and well-balanced, with velvety tannins, and a fresh and remarkably aromatic finish.

*FOOD PAIRINGS:* Syrah might be known as the quintessential "big red" wine, calling to be paired with red meats and other hearty fare—from beef and lamb to tuna, goose, and game, or fattier cuts of pork. It's great with grilled, roasted, or braised meats and mature cheeses.

And while grilling or roasting are always good preparation ideas when serving Syrah, try bringing out the sweetly scented berry or plum qualities of Syrah by first marinating any number of ways. We've had luck with soy sauces infused with ginger, garlic, scallions, star anise, lemongrass, and even chili pastes, balanced by sweeteners like palm sugar (ah, the Chinese- or Asian-fusion-friendly elements of Syrah).

And yes, Syrah is wonderful with lamb (just like Shiraz), especially grilled or roasted with rosemary and garlic, or perhaps paired with a mint risotto. If you can find them, try goat shanks instead of lamb—wonderful in the crock pot, braised with onions and garlic, tomatoes, and some beef stock and a little red wine, cooked until it falls delectably off the bone.

For a real taste of Italy, try this Syrah with a beef brasato (beef braised in red wine) with pappardelle and mint. Marinate beef shanks, oxtails, or short ribs overnight in red wine with some mint sprigs. Drain, reserving the marinade, and remove the mint. Pat the beef dry and brown in oil. Place browned beef, wine marinade, and a large can of tomatoes into a large dutch oven, bring to a boil on the stove top, and then transfer to a 325 degree oven. Cook for about two and a half hours, or until the meat is very tender. Transfer the meat to a bowl or platter, remove the bones, and shred the meat. Reduce the braising liquid by boiling for about twenty minutes. Cook the pappardelle to al dente, drain, and return to the pot. Add the meat and the reduced braising liquid, stirring over heat for about two minutes to coat the pasta. In a small skillet, heat some oil, add a couple garlic cloves, heat for about one minute, and then toss in some fresh mint leaves. Cook for a few seconds, and pour this over the pasta and meat.

Vegetarian? Try this lovely Syrah with Moroccan vegetable stew, portabella burgers, or perhaps a hearty lentil soup or warm lentil salad with mushrooms, tomatoes, and black olives.

# Tuscan Rosé

Not sure you'll like a rosé wine? Try a Tuscan rosé—a lovely dry wine usually created from Sangiovese grapes and perhaps another varietal, such as Merlot, Cabernet Sauvignon, or Syrah. It is definitely *not* a white Zinfandel! No "fruit punch" profile, not sweet and simple.

Rosé wine is one of the oldest varieties of wine, produced by the Greeks twenty-six centuries ago. However, when the Romans superseded the Greeks in Italy, they preferred red wine over rosé, leaving the juice on the pressed grape skins until the color was bold and dark red. "Pink wine" (rosé) fell by the wayside in Italian wine making, only recently coming back into favor.

Rosé wine can be made in two ways. Most Tuscan rosé is made by using the "maceration method"—the red grapes are pressed, and after a few hours, the juice is separated from the skins and then fermented. (In making red wine, the juice and skins are left together through fermentation.) Both the variety of the grapes used and the length of time the juice remains with the skins determines the color of the resulting rosé wine.

The second method is known as "saignee." It is a by-product of making some red wines. After the grapes are pressed, some of the juice is bled off so that the percentage of juice to skins is lower, and the resulting red wine will be darker, richer, and bolder. The bled-off juice or "saignee" is then refermented into rosé. Wines made in this way are generally a deeper, darker pink than those made by the maceration method, and they also have a greater depth of flavor.

Tuscan rosés—*vino rosato* or *Rosato di Toscana*, as they are known—are crisp, and the fresh red-cherry taste of the Sangiovese grapes comes through strongly. Drunk unusually cold by Tuscan standards, these wines are almost all an excellent accompaniment to lunch "under the Tuscan sun" when a cold, low-alcohol glass of wine goes perfectly with the classic combination of prosciutto, mozzarella, and a slice of melon, or perhaps onion soup garnished with gorgonzola and prosciutto.

# Real Men Do Drink Pink—Inspired by Ceppaiano Rosé Toscano

Let me acquaint you with a Tuscan take on rosé wine, from Sangiovese and Syrah grapes. It's a lovely color and flavor, a wonderful dry rosé, perfect for sipping or with appetizers. Not just for the ladies…

**STORY:** Summertime. Thoughts of beaches and vacations, long dinners under the stars, with family and good friends, and good food and great wine. Trust me; this is a little of what goes though the mind of an Italian at this time of year.

And so, Paolo and I are in Viareggio, one of the oldest and most famous seaside resorts in Tuscany. Viareggio is known as much for its excellent cuisine and exciting nightlife as for the wide, sandy beaches that fall gently into the Mediterranean Sea. We are sitting in one of the many cafés on the promenade the runs along the beach. The air is perfumed with the scent of salt and the pine forests that shelter the town.

Paolo has lived in this area most of his life.

"When I was little," he says, "I remember spending some of my summer holidays here. I would swim and play, but when I was tired, and my parents wanted to sit and relax, they gave me a time-consuming chore that kept me out of trouble and happily busy—digging in the sand and finding *arselle* or *telline*. This also gave me a culinary focus and goal.

"You see," Paolo explains, "arselle, telline, or zighe are tiny clams found in some areas of coastal Tuscany, including here in the Viareggio area. They are small but have a distinct flavor, and if you're patient enough to collect quite a few, the resulting recipe is unforgettable.

"See," he continues, "here it is on the menu, in the traditional manner, arselle with garlic and tomatoes. And you must try the *cacciucco*, our Tuscan seafood stew, full of all the bounty of the sea. And the *spaghetti alla trabaccolara*—the pasta will be as the fresh as the fish the sauce is made with. It takes its name from the *trabaccolara*, the name of the boats of the local fishermen, who prepared a sauce, simple yet perfectly delicious, on board the boat or right on the shore, from the leftover fish that they could not sell."

Paolo adds caponata to our dinner order, in memory of his grandmother who was from Sicily and made this eggplant dish often, and veal carpaccio, "simply because it's so good in the summer." I have to agree, although I happen to know it was created in Venice, not in Tuscany, in 1950, by Giuseppe Cipriani, the owner of the famous Harry's Bar, for a countess. It seems our meal will literally span Italy.

I wonder what my soccer-playing, motorcycle-riding friend has ordered to drink with dinner—perhaps beer? It's summer; we have beef and fish, some spicy, some not. "Oh, no," he says, and assures me he has found the perfect wine to accompany what promises to be a most memorable meal. "It is from a vineyard not far from here, on the banks of River Arno, near Cascina. You remember Cascina. It's between Florence and Pisa."

I nod, vaguely remembering seeing the sign on our drive to the coast.

"*The Battle of Cascin*a—one of Michelangelo's famous 'lost works'—it was commissioned by a Florentine statesman in honor of one of Florence's notable victories over the rival city-state of Pisa, but never completed, and only copies of Michelangelo's drawings, and a few individual sketches, exist."

I wonder how a macho guy like Paolo knows this. Maybe it has to do with being Italian.

The wine arrives first, our aperitivo. It is a very cold bottle of rosé, from Tenuta di Ceppaiano (Estate Ceppaiano). It seems real men do drink rosé.

"Rosé wine," Paolo explains, "can be traced back to ancient Greece, when much of the red wine produced was pale red. You see, wine was not left to macerate on the skins for as long as it does today and, thus, never became fully red. It was our Roman ancestors who popularized darker red wines. So today we have a relative scarcity of Italian rosé wines, compared to reds, unlike France, where the Greeks introduced wine making to Provence some twenty-six centuries ago, and their traditions, not the Romans', continued. Provence is still famous for rosé wines today. But Italy is gaining, with rosé wines like this Rosato di Toscana."

We raise our glasses. The wine is, indeed, perfect for the entire meal. Dry, fruity, yet with a slightly minerally or herbal quality that is refreshing and savory. Almost salty. "Ah, yes," Paolo says, "you can taste the Mediterranean breezes over the vineyard, and the marine fossils in the soil.

"I like to think," says Paolo, "that Lorenzo de Medici, Lorenzo the Magnificent, and perhaps Michelangelo and Leonardo da Vinci, who loved good wine and lived in this area, would have enjoyed a wine like this. Who knows, perhaps they did. It is made from one of Italy's oldest grapes, the Sangiovese. And what could be more macho than drinking 'Jove's blood,' which is the literal translation of Sangiovese, even if it is pink?"

**DESCRIPTION:** Rosé wine is one of the oldest varieties of wine, produced by the Greeks twenty-six centuries ago. Dry rosé wines, like the Ceppaiano Rosé Toscana from the Sangiovese grape, could be thought of as the sophisticated summer sisters of many red wine varietals. They retain the true flavor of the grapes from which they are made, but they are more subtle. They are ideal to enjoy during the summer months, while you're outside enjoying the sun, or in the winter to help brighten a gloomy day. And they complement a wide variety of foods.

The Ceppaiano vineyard is located on the edges of the Arno River, not far from Pisa and the sea, on sandy soils rich in minerals and fossils of marine origin. The vineyard employs organic cultivation techniques and carefully hand-harvests the grapes. Ceppaiano Rosé is lovingly crafted using 90 percent Sangiovese grapes, with 10 percent Syrah. The vinification cellars are right in the vineyard, preserving the freshness and pureness of the fruit. Each varietal is individually fermented at no more than sixty five degrees Fahrenheit, and then blended, and the wine is kept at low temperatures to preserve the characteristic aromas and flavors.

Rosé wines from Tuscany still tend to be somewhat rare, and this one is a true treasure. Ceppaiano wines are juicy, luscious, and mouthwatering.

Serve this wine nicely chilled, whether on a summer day or in front of a winter fire.

**TASTING NOTES:** The flavors of rosé wines tends to be more subtle versions of their red-wine varietal counterparts. The fruit expectations lean toward strawberry, cherry, and raspberry, with some notes of apple, citrus, and watermelon. The Sangiovese grape's signature herbal and violet scent adds a lovely savory note to the dryish cherry and apple flavors of this wine. The terroir of the vineyard is reflected in a delicate and appealingly saline taste as well, reflecting the warm climate, Mediterranean breezes, and marine fossils in the soil.

Ceppaiano Rosé is a beautifully intense but light pink color, with slight hints of purple, as you swirl it in your glass. Perhaps the scent will remind you, as it does Paolo and I, of the Mediterranean seacoast. The bouquet combines fruit—peach, plum, apricot, cherries, and raspberries—with herbal notes and fresh spring violets.

You taste and think…"Yes, complexity and concentration of flavors, yet so easy to drink. What are those flavors? Wild berries, strawberries, and cherries? A hint of peach and pink grapefruit? Almond? Spice? And the savory, mouthwatering essence of the sea."

**FOOD PAIRINGS:** Ceppaiano Rosé Toscano is ideal as an aperitif or companion to so very many foods. Serve it with most appetizers, entrée salads, grilled poultry, fish, and lighter fare.

Of course, it's perfect with Tuscan seafood dishes, such as spaghetti alla trabaccolara (spaghetti, preferably freshly made, with fresh fish sauce—onions and garlic, some fresh tomatoes, white wine, and of course, a variety of fresh fish); arsella or telline (tiny clams) steamed on a bed of garlic and tomatoes; and cacciucco, a peppery seafood stew—various kinds of fish, clams or mussels, shrimp, and calamari or octopus, and redolent with garlic, tomatoes, and peppers.

For an unlikely match, but one made in heaven, try this with pork or chicken stir-fry.

Ceppaiano Rosé is also wonderful with "small plates" in the Mediterranean style, including Turkish food and Spanish tapas.

And it's the perfect go-to wine for summer meals. If you are opting for surf and turf, rest assured that this rosé can handle both the seafood and the steak in one fell sip. It's also a great picnic wine, as it tends to have both a lighter body and more delicate flavors on the palate, presenting a great wine partner for a ham, chicken, or roast-beef sandwiches, along with a fruit, potato, or egg salad. It can even handle a variety of chips and dips. Ceppaiano Rosé is also the perfect guest to bring to a backyard barbecue, tackling hamburgers, hot dogs, and even french fries and ketchup with ease and aplomb.

# Brunello (Sangiovese's Elegant Big Brother)

There is a mystique to the name of Brunello, tradition and prestige behind the name, and a reputation of being the best of the best. Those who know wine rank Brunello di Montalcino as one of world's greatest red wines, not just one of Italy's best.

Brunello di Montalcino is a red Italian wine produced in the vineyards surrounding the town of Montalcino located about 75 miles south of Florence in the Tuscany wine region. Brunello, roughly translated as "little brown one" in the local dialect, is the unofficial name of the clone of Sangiovese (also known as Sangiovese Grosso) grown in the Montalcino region.

The small commune of Montalcino has always made very good wines from the Sangiovese grape. Only about thirty miles from the Tyrrhenian Sea, warm breezes flow up the river valleys to the vineyards on the hills, giving Montalcino the warmest and driest climate in Tuscany. This, combined with the altitude of the hills and the variety of soils, allows the grapes to ripen more fully and consistently than anywhere else in Tuscany. These factors contribute to the body, color, complexity, flavors, and tannins that characterize Brunello di Montalcino, brought out to perfection by the artistry of the winemaker.

The first mention of "Brunello" wine dates from the fourteenth century, but this "ancestor" of today's Brunello was a very different wine, although a very good one according to historical accounts. Vineyards in Montalcino continued to produce excellent red wines using this name up through the 1800s. The origin of "modern" Brunello can be traced to the mid-1800s and one vintner, Ferruccio Biondi-Santi, whose estate was just outside the beautiful little medieval hill town of Montalcino.

Following the dreams of his grandfather to produce the best wine in Italy, a wine made from 100 percent of the local Sangiovese Grosso grape that could be aged for a long time, Biondi-Santi isolated a subvariety (clone) of Sangiovese Grosso, known as "Brunello" for its dark-brownish skin. Because this specific variety not only produced exceptional wine, but was also resistant to phylloxera, Biondi-Santi planted his entire vineyard with these vines. He also continued his grandfather's experimentation with wine-making techniques, giving the musts lengthy maceration and extended aging in large oak casks known as botte. His goal was to produce an exceptional wine, age-worthy and concentrated. Biondi-Santi succeeded admirably, and legendary wines were made in 1888 and again in 1891.

The first great vintage, officially, was the 1888 Brunello. Remarkably, five bottles still exist. Their contents are perfectly preserved, proof of the wine's great powers of longevity. With the passing of the years, it steadily acquires greater fragrance, a more velvety flavor, increased harmony, and an odor that is delicate and at the same time quite intense.

Brunello di Montalcino has always been a rare treasure. There were only four vintages—1888, 1891, 1925, and 1945—declared in the first fifty-seven years of production, and in 1960, there were only eleven producers. The few bottles that had slipped into distribution were cherished by wine connoisseurs and collectors for their uncompromising depth, longevity, and high price.

While there were only a handful of small Brunello estates in 1970s, Brunello di Montalcino was nonetheless the first wine to be awarded the coveted DOCG designation (denominazione di origine controllata e garantitia), an official recognition of the significance and quality of the wine, in 1980.

Today, Brunello di Montalcino is thankfully more available, though still a rare treasure. The number of producers of the wine has grown to more than two hundred; these wineries produce some 330,000 to 350,000 cases of the Brunello wine annually. (To lend a sense of scale, consider that the region's total annual Brunello production is easily dwarfed by the output of a single, medium-sized winery in California.)

By the end of World War II, Brunello di Montalcino had developed a reputation as one of Italy's rarest and best wines, a treasure.

During my time in Italy, I was fortunate to sample several bottles of this legendary wine and attend the annual "Benvenuto Brunello" event where the new vintage is released and graded.

# A Wine for Meditation — Inspired by Brunello di Montalcino, Cava d'Onice

**STORY:** I sit in front of the fireplace, lost in the flickering reflection of dancing flames and the lush red wine in my glass. It is, as the Italians say, "vino da meditazione" ("a wine for meditation"), and, I would add, for memories— either making them or recalling the best of them, with someone as special as this wine. And so it is that I remember my first visit to Val d'Orcia, the Valley of the Orcia River, and my introduction to this king of Italian wines, Brunello di Montalcino.

It was a cool, almost cold, foggy winter day in Tuscany. Branches still holding orange persimmons swayed slightly in a gentle wind. The color palette of the hills had shifted from the golds of summer to the shockingly bright greens that appear in Tuscany only in the winter and early spring. Soft gray fog rolled slowly across the valley, pierced by the tall cypress trees, and a blanket of silence suggested a landscape that had gone into hibernation. Medieval villages lay like slumbering animals, curled on the hilltops, sand-colored stone and worn cobblestone paths shrouded in misty rain. Yesterday's walk in the forest had flushed pheasant and hare and even a family of wild boar, rarely seen in the summer, but almost expected on quiet winter walks. Of such things are poems and novels inspired, as well as romance.

This was the undiscovered Tuscany, waiting to be found. This was the real Tuscany, Paolo told me, Tuscany in the dead of winter, Tuscany with virtually no tourists, a Tuscany populated only by Tuscans.

Lunchtime found Paolo and me in Sant'Angelo in Colle, one of those tiny Montalcino villages that seem to have been lifted out of a Renaissance painting, in perhaps its most well-known trattoria. Casual, yet sporting starched tablecloths and crystal wine glasses befitting the great wines from the area, the menu is local Tuscan fare, and the legendary wine cellar is stocked with well over four thousand bottles. Il Leccio is also the unofficial cantina of Tuscany's greatest wine producers.

On that winter day, several tables were occupied by some of those winery owners and vintners, some young, some gray-haired. Our waiter recommended a fifteen-year-old Brunello di Montalcino, made by one of the vintners at the next table, to accompany our lunch of melt-in-the-mouth cinghale (wild boar) stew, accented with porcini mushrooms. That was our introduction to Brunello, and we've been aficionados ever since. One sip, and we had to agree—this was, indeed, one of the best red wines in the world.

Paolo took a sip and proclaimed it "Beethoven's *Ninth Symphony* in liquid form…" I think he meant it was a luscious, complex, harmonious, powerful, and elegant wine that transcended, like the Beethoven's *Ninth*, from the terrestrial to the divine.

With that compliment, Paolo struck up a conversation with the vintners, and soon we were learning some of the history of this wine, Montalcino, and the winery, Cava d'Onice, which produced the wine we were savoring.

**DESCRIPTION:** Brunello di Montalcino is simply a magnificent red wine, one of the best in the world, often compared to the best Burgundy has to offer.

Crafted from carefully selected Brunello grapes, the wine goes through an extended maceration period where color and flavor are extracted from the skins. Following fermentation, the wine is then aged in oak for a minimum of two years. It is then transferred to bottles for additional aging and is finally released in January of the fifth year after grape harvest.

You can enjoy this Brunello when it is released (five years after vintage), but it also has the structure to age well, unlike most Sangiovese-based wines. On average, ten years after the vintage is a good time to enjoy them, and the wine should continue to improve for another several years.

To fully appreciate this wine, I suggest you open and decant it at least four hours before serving. Serve at sixty-four to sixty-eight degrees Fahrenheit (too warm or too cool will take away from the taste), in good crystal balloon wine glasses, as it deserves.

**TASTING NOTES:** Your bottle of Cava d'Onice Brunello di Montalcino has been opened and decanted. It has been breathing for a good four hours, and its flavors and aromas are now fully alive. It's ready for you to enjoy, at the perfect temperature.

Each vintage and each producer's wines are unique, reflecting the terroir, the weather, and the vision of the vintner. And of course the wine will change as it slowly matures.

What can you expect, no matter the vintage?

The wine will be a beautiful ruby-red color in your glass, with a translucent golden edge, befitting the treasure it is. As you swirl the glass, enticing aromas of dried flowers, berries, and licorice or balsamic notes meet your nose. Perhaps you'll detect scents of wild roses and iris and lavender, and cherries and roasted chestnuts, along with a hint of the good red earth of Montalcino after a summer rain.

The taste is complex and rich, with fine tannins and a long, silky finish, at once forceful yet elegant, subtle, and caressing. So many layers and facets…sweetness of fruit—blackberries and raspberries predominate—and wild roses; components of earth and spice—anise, juniper, briar, tobacco, mineral, and balsamic notes. Taste this, and you just might agree with the Italians, who consider Brunello a "vino da meditazione," because it's so complex and structured a wine that it can be enjoyed without food, enjoyed with full attention and devotion to appreciating its flavors and composition.

Here are my impressions of the 2006 and 2007 vintages, both five-star. Our favorite was the 2007.

The 2006 vintage has higher acidity and a long aging potential, somewhat sharper, linear, and more austere…a very powerful, aristocratic, masculine wine.

The 2007 vintage, on the other hand, delivers buxom beauty with softer lines, enormous richness, impressive structure, and opulence in the mouth. The acidity is not as sharp as 2006. The 2007 presents strong cola or menthol-like notes of licorice, dried ginger, cured meat, and white pepper, or as the Italians refer to these characteristics, *note balsamiche*. These delicate and compelling aromas are unique to Sangiovese, especially when the summer is dry but not overly warm, as 2007 was.

The fruit component in this vintage is rich with crème de cassis, black currant, and wild berry. While past vintages have been dominated by bold cherry, the 2007 is definitely more nuanced. These wines are ready to drink sooner than is typical for the wines of the region, but they also show excellent aging potential because of their firm, velvety structure. The tannic ripeness makes them generous and approachable.

Cava d'Onice has also just released the 2010 vintages. The 2010 vintage (a five-star year) displays aromas of dark fruit, walnut, dried spices, and some wet earth and orange peel. It needs two or three years to soften, but it is already beautiful.

**FOOD PAIRINGS:** Brunello di Montalcino can be enjoyed on its own as a "vino da meditazione," savoring and focusing on all its complexity and depth of flavor, but it is a magnificent wine for a very special dinner.

The elegance, depth, and structure of this wine make it an excellent accompaniment to many complex and complicated dishes of many cuisines, not just Italian. Think chateaubriand or beef Wellington—exquisite!

In Italy, Brunello is considered the classic wine to drink with stewed or roasted cinghiale (wild boar) or rabbit ragù over pappardelle, or cheeses such as aged parmesan or Tuscan pecorino.

We love it with a roasted pork loin, served with garlic mashed potatoes or creamy polenta and wild mushrooms, or roast leg of lamb, crusted with Tuscan herbs and garlic, done to medium rare, served with oven-roasted potatoes and lightly steamed green beans. Another great pairing for this wine is roast duck.

It's also perfect with any sultry braised meat-shank dish. Try lamb shanks, braised and roasted to melt-in-your-mouth perfection, perhaps with a savory coffee-based glaze.

Brunello di Montalcino is, for some, the ultimate wine for grilled steak, and Tuscany's beef is indeed the finest in Italy, as exemplified by bistecca alla fiorentina from Chianana cattle. Here in the United States, we suggest you select the very best steak from your local butcher, such as a one-inch-thick rib eye or filet mignon, and cook it Florentine style—grilled with salt and pepper, maybe some rosemary and garlic, to rare perfection. Who says simple isn't sexy?

Vegetarian? Marinated and grilled portabello mushrooms over polenta is another excellent partner.

# Of Bentleys, Breitlings, and Brunello — Inspired by Brunello di Montalcino Riserva, Cava d'Onice

*When only the very best will do—this is the red wine to serve. A rare treasure in numbered bottles, Brunello di Montalcino Riserva is truly a wine for the ages.*

**STORY:** On very, very special occasions, I indulge in a bottle of Brunello di Montalcino Riserva. It is shared with only our very best friends, who will appreciate it for the treasure it is. Most often, though, it is shared with a very special someone. We feel so very special, so privileged, almost like royalty when we sip this wine. We feel almost like that wealthy couple we met at "Benvuto Brunello."

Their car, a classic older Bentley.

Their watches, Breitlings.

The champagne they serve before dinner? Bollinger Les Vieilles Vignes Francaises, a Blanc de Noir, produced from ungrafted Pinot Noir vines grown on three tiny, exceptional plots.

The caviar would of course be beluga, were its importation not prohibited. Karaburun Ossetra cavier from a similar variety of sturgeon found in the southern Caspian, a mere $1100 for a nine-ounce tin, has been deemed an acceptable substitute.

The beef, exquisitely grilled filet mignon, is Kobe.

And the red wine served with this dinner? It's a Brunello di Montalcino Riserva, selected from their extensive cellar. Produced in very limited quantities, and only in the best vintage years, Brunello di Montalcino Riserva is one of the world's best red wines, a rare and exquisite treasure. Many producers individually number each precious bottle.

This elegant couple travel to Montalcino, Italy, each February, attend the "by invitation only" event "Benvenuto Brunello" where the release of the next vintage of Brunello and Brunello Riserva occurs, and visit their favorite wineries. In five-star vintage years, they will select wines from the best pro-ducers to ship home to add to their cellar. Of the past twenty vintages released (1990—2010), only seven have been awarded five stars.

Paolo's uncle is their wine contact for Italy. Every year he manages an invitation to this event for Paolo, and this year for me as well. We are introduced to this American couple and soon are discussing wine and wineries.

We discover we have something in common—a few years ago they, too, discovered Cava d'Onice and its Brunello wines. Their cellar now contains Brunello di Montalcino Reservas from Cava d'Onice, as well as other select favorite vineyards.

Each year, when they receive their shipment of wine, they host a small, intimate dinner and wine tasting to celebrate the arrival of the new Brunello. They open a bottle from each of several older vintages for comparison. The discussion, among the cherished friends and wine lovers present, will be how these vintages compare, and how the new release will age and mature over the next four to forty years. I am flattered and somewhat amazed when they promise me and Paolo an invitation to this dinner when I am back in the States. Oh, my, whatever shall I wear?

If you are lucky, perhaps you too can secure an invitation to the annual Brunello event, or discover a new winery and young vintner with great prom-ise, who grew up in the vineyards and the wineries, learning the art and craft of wine making from some of the best in Montalcino. If you do, don't hesi-tate: there may only be five hundred individually numbered bottles available. Perhaps you don't have a Bentley yet, or even a Breitling, but you too can have treasure in your cellar, like I do, a precious few of those beautiful numbered bottles of a Brunello di Montalcino Riserva.

**DESCRIPTION:** Brunello di Montalcino Riserva—the best of the best red wine in the world. This wine is produced only in the best years, and in very limited quantities, as the vintners hand-select grapes from the best and rip-est bunches of Brunello, the special varietal of the Sangiovese Grosso grape grown in Montalcino, from the best of their vineyards.

Simone Nannutti, owner of Cava d'Onice, had produced only five hundred numbered bottles of the highly rated 2006 Brunello di Montalcino Riserva, and a similar number of the 2007 vintage. When I found Cava d'Onice, only a few remained available for purchase by knowledgeable wine aficionados, making this a wine that will surely appreciate in value, as well as improve in taste. James Suckling, renowned wine critic, awarded the 2006 93 points and the 2007 94 points, saying, "What a wonderful texture to this wine, with creamy tannins and delicious fruit. Full body, with silky tannins and a juicy finish. Delicious now, but will improve with age." I'm eagerly awaiting release of the 2010 vintage.

This Brunello wine is aged in oak for a period of five years according to regulations: four years in French and Slavonia oak barrels of small capacity, and twelve months in the bottle, in a temperature-controlled environment. This allows the Riserva the time it needs to release tannins. It is released for sale in the sixth year after vintage.

The five-star 2006 vintage produced big, structured wines with higher acidity; streamlined, elegant wines with enormous potential for long cellar aging. While this vintage could have been enjoyed when it was released in 2011, it should be aged for another five to ten years, at a minimum. It's a jewel of a wine, a treasure, with anticipated maturity from 2016 to 2046. The 2007 vintage, also awarded five stars, was even better, with big, luscious flavor and elegance, described as a "beautifully layered, expressive wine, caressing the palate with exceptional elegance, finesse and total class. A radiant Brunello."

I recommend opening and decanting this wine at least eight hours before serving; serve at sixty-two to sixty-eight degrees Fahrenheit, in elegant crystal balloon glasses.

***TASTING NOTES:*** This Cava d'Onice Brunello Riserva has been described by connoisseurs as "powerful, even virile, yet elegant, refined and sophisticated." One of our female friends sighed, "If only I could find a man like this…" One taste, and you too will understand why this Brunello di Montalcino Riserva is rated as one of the best red wines in the world, in the rarified company of the very best from Bordeaux.

Cava d'Onice Brunello Riserva glows in your glass—an intense ruby red, with garnet undertones, befitting the treasured jewel it is. Swirl it in your goblet, and inhale deeply. The bouquet, a preview of the taste, is full and harmonic, a complex symphony—wild berries and plums, spices and roasted coffee, dried meadow flowers, and leather and tobacco. It has a full, well-developed, rich structure, with tannins that grow even richer as it ages. It is smooth, warm, and well-balanced, with a long, elegant, and silky finish. This, you will think, is exactly how a red wine should taste.

**FOOD PAIRINGS:** This is a wine for special occasions, to complement food as good as it is—the highest quality, well prepared. Truly a wine to savor while dining, even if you are not dressed to the nines.

The food pairings for Cava d'Onice Brunello Riserva should be in line with its elevated stature—elegant, sophisticated, refined. We love it with the traditional "Fiorentina" T-bone steak, grilled to rare perfection, succulent osso buco, or savory veal piccata, or a thick, tender filet mignon, a standing rib roast, or beef Wellington. And of course, it complements the traditional foods of Tuscany, especially dishes prepared with wild boar, suckling pig, or game. For a very special and unique dinner, serve this Brunello di Montalcino Riserva with roast pheasant for a meal befitting nobility. It also pairs well with very mature cheeses, such as parmigiano reggiano, Tuscan pecorino, provolone, and Castelmagno.

# Rosso di Montalcino
## The Affordable Charms of Montalcino — Inspired by Cava d'Onice Rosso di Montalcino

*The perfect fall red wine—warm, smooth, fruity, and spicy. Crafted from the famous Sangiovese Brunello grape, this is pure Montalcino, minus the wait—more approachable, more affordable.*

**STORY:** Tuscany in the fall is breathtakingly beautiful. Imagine New England fall colors, ancient villas, hilltop castles. The grape harvest just finishing. It's also hunting season, so succulent, rich dishes from wild boar and game birds abound. And then of course, there are the wonderful red wines, warm and smooth, perfect for this season.

Walking is a wonderful way to see Tuscany, to experience it by immersion—the colors, the smells, the sights, the people, the food, and the wine. You come to know it intimately. Come with me on a fall ramble through the south of Tuscany, in an area famed for world-class wines and one of the most photographed chapels in all of Italy.

One of the many small towns in the beautiful Val d'Orcia, Montalcino stands proud atop a hill. Montalcino is a classic fairy-tale hilltop town, set within a full circle of fortified walls and watched over by a mighty castle of medieval perfection. Visiting is like stepping inside an Italian Renaissance painting. The town has scarcely changed in appearance since the sixteenth century. The labyrinthine narrow streets and alleys are still paved with stone, and around every corner are cafés and restaurants, small shops of all kinds, and places to buy wine.

The central fortress dates from 1361, dominating both the town and the surrounding hills, which are planted with vineyards. Today this castle serves as an elegant wine-tasting center for tourists and visitors. Paolo and I walk the bastions, admiring the view, nibbling on ossi di morto, the traditional biscotti-like cookies that are made here in Montalcino, and sipping wine, a local Rosso di Montalcino.

The town is surrounded by the breathtaking Val d'Orcia National Park. The view from the fortress walls is magnificent—rolling, sunny hills awash with yellow and red flowers, ancient oak trees, picturesque olive groves, scenic country roads winding through perfect vineyards, and isolated cypress trees atop hills.

From Montalcino, it's a short walk to the magnificent Abbey of Sant'Antimo, just outside of town. Founded by Charlemagne in 781, it's a rare example of French-Romanesque architecture, with a gracefully curved apse. Built of travertine and onyx from the many quarries in the surrounding area, in certain lights, the abbey seems to glow from within. We have timed our visit perfectly, it seems; we experience a truly magical, spiritual experience, transported to another time, listening to the resident monks sing traditional Gregorian chants.

After a reverent hour, Paolo and I tear ourselves away. I want a few photos of Cappella di Vitaleta. This tiny chapel can be reached only on foot. Just south of Montalcino, Cappella di Vitaleta stands in the middle of a field, flanked by two rows of towering cypress trees. It is reportedly the most photographed church in Tuscany, and perhaps in all of Italy. In the fall, you might be the only one visiting this iconic landmark, as Paolo and I were. The surrounding fields glow golden and green in the sun, the cypress trees vibrant green, the sky several shades of bright blue, punctuated by high white clouds.

All this walking and beauty will no doubt have given you an appetite, as it does us, which the restaurants in and around Montalcino can more than satisfy. A couple of our favorites include Taverna Grappolo Blu and Osteria di Porta al Cassero.

Taverna Grappolo Blu is tucked down the Via Mazzini but easily located by the wonderful aromas drifting from Maria Pia's kitchen. Head down the stairs and join the other happy diners at bare wooden tables—will you have the pinci (thick, hand-rolled spaghetti that is a local specialty and addiction) with meat sauce and mushrooms or "all aglione" (with whole cloves of garlic and cherry tomatoes), or the rabbit in Brunello sauce, with an obligatory side order of cannellini beans?

Located a two-minute walk from the fortezza, Osteria di Porta al Cassero is easy to find. In the fall, Paolo and I especially like their wild-boar stew, which is served with tiny, delicious white Tuscan beans, or the local version of liver and onions, where the onions are cooked in tomato sauce—the result is superb. And of course, with any of these, we share a bottle of the delightful local red wine, Rosso di Montalcino, warm, fruity, spicy, and smooth.

Wine has been made here since the area was settled by the Etruscans and Romans, who also mined the precious local onyx, carving beautiful cameos from the black-and-cream or brown-and-cream translucent stone. The excellent wines produced around Montalcino have been prized for centuries, and they have contributed to making this town famous throughout the world. In the early 1980s, Montalcino vintners developed a more approachable and more affordable wine from these Brunello grapes—Rosso di Montalcino—that can be enjoyed just two years after vintage. It's a wonderful wine in its own right, one to enjoy any time with friends, not just reserved for very special occasions as its "big brother" Brunello di Montalcino usually is.

Our walking adventures in Montalcino also afford the opportunity to visit some of the two hundred wineries that craft wines from these Brunello grapes, to appreciate the care and traditions of the winemakers, to understand the skill and the art of making these fine wines, and the love of the land and the vines that all these vintners share, as well as each one's individual vision and passion for the wines they create. And yes, to sample them. In the fall, we can share in the joys of the harvest, the sights and sounds and smells of the crush, and the promise the vintage holds. Many are small, boutique wineries, crafting exceptional, award-winning wine in small quantities, rarely available outside the local area. One of these is Cava d'Onice, whose wines we fell in love with. The winery name means "Onyx Quarry," a nod to history and a nearby ancient quarry.

Savoring a glass of Rosso di Montalcino with friends in the fall, with a hearty soup, pasta, or stew, will transport you, as it does me, back to Tuscany and Montalcino. It's the perfect fall red wine, and to be honest, it's a wine that pairs well with a good Sunday football game on TV, too.

**DESCRIPTION:** Rosso di Montalcino might be the perfect fall wine – smooth, warm, elegant and an excellent complement to so many fall meals. It has been called "baby Brunello" and "pure Montalcino, minus the wait" – but these monikers scarcely do it justice.

Made from the same grapes from the same area as that world-class Italian red, Brunello di Montalcino, Rosso di Montalcino is soulful, elemental—like good trattoria food. Made from a local cultivar of the Sangiovese grape, known locally as "Brunello," it is full of the unmistakably earthy, dusty flavors of pure Sangiovese, with winsome, citrus-tinged cherry flavors.

The Cava d'Onice winery has vineyards in some of the best areas around Montalcino, with a variety of exposures and soils lending complexity to the wines. The winery's name hearkens back to Etruscan and Roman times and the onyx quarry nearby, which provided stone for jewelry as well as buildings. The young owner and vintner, Simone Manneti, comes from a long line of wine producers, having learned the art from his father and grandfather. His love of the land and artistry with these grapes is evident in every bottle, and by the awards Cava d'Onice wines have won.

The Brunello grapes are carefully hand-harvested and softly pressed. After the initial fermentation, the wine is aged for one year in French oak barrels before release. The result is a lovely red wine—warm, soft, velvety, retaining the fruity notes Sangiovese is known for, mellowed by the oak. While Rosso di Montalcino is meant to be enjoyed upon release, it can also be aged for several years, mellowing and improving.

I recommend you uncork this Rosso at least four hours before pouring to allow the wine to open to its full luscious potential. Serve at about sixty-five to sixty-eight degrees Fahrenheit in large red-wine goblets.

**TASTING NOTES:** This Rosso di Montalcino is a brilliant ruby red with a bright and good texture. The nose opens with notes of blackberries and black cherries followed by hints of flowery violet and spices, ending with notes of coffee and licorice.

Warm and soft to the taste, Cava d'Onice Rosso has a velvety balance with good structure and tannins. Echoing the nose, the palate is succulent black cherries and wild-fruit berries, with spice and vanilla overtones from the careful use of oak. The finish is lingering and pleasant with a persistent fruity aftertaste.

As Paolo says, "Brunello is a wine for thinking; this Rosso is a wine for drinking!"

**FOOD PAIRINGS:** Cava d'Onice Rosso di Montalcino is such a smooth, luscious wine that it can be enjoyed alone, but like all Italian wines, it's meant to be enjoyed with food. With its medium body, smooth, elegant taste of cherries and spice, and velvety tannins, this is a versatile wine that pairs well with a wide variety of dishes and cuisines, from hearty soups or buttery, rich pastas, to grilled tenderloin with herb sauce, to chicken and game.

It goes perfectly with a classic Tuscany antipasto, of course, and almost all semihard cheeses. Try it with Tuscan classics, such as pasta puttanesca (a spicy, fast, and easy pasta sauce featuring garlic, anchovy, black olives, capers, crushed and diced tomatoes, and fresh parsley and basil) or pasta with pancetta, tomato, and white-wine sauce.

This Rosso also works well with poultry, pork, and veal, especially with sauces including mushrooms or truffles. Our vegetarian friends love it with hearty vegetarian lasagna or creamy mushroom risotto.

It has the structure to stand up to and enhance roast beef and fall stews, especially a savory lamb or wild-boar stew (look for boar in your specialty butcher shop). No wild boar? Try some goat or pork shoulder in the stew instead.

One of our favorite fall recipes is cassoulet, the traditional Southern French white-bean-based stew. Its combination of creamy, protein-rich beans; savory pork shoulder; luxurious and a touch gamy duck confit; and Provençal herbs might even make you glad it's cold outside. This Rosso is the perfect partner for a cassoulet, as well as more traditional Tuscan white-bean recipes.

For something simpler than cassoulet, we love white-bean soups. Onions, a little Parmigiano cheese rind, rosemary, and lacinato kale add depth to some of our favorite Tuscan white-bean soup recipes, and many don't require anything you don't have in your fridge or pantry. Or add some browned Italian sausage for a hearty "eat-with-a-fork" soup. Truly comfort food, with an international flair.

And for an easy but sophisticated appetizer to serve at your next party, mash up or puree some cooked white beans with roasted garlic, chopped rosemary, and red chili-pepper flakes, season to taste, and slather across grilled artisan bread like Pugliese or pane integrale. Open a bottle of Rosso di Montalcino, and stand by for compliments.

# Region: Umbria

**Wines:**
- **White Blend**
- **Red Blends**
- **Pinot Grigio**

**Wineries:**
- **Cirulli**
- **Ganzo**

# Umbria

⎯⎯⎯⎯ ⎯⎯⎯⎯

BORDERING TUSCANY, UMBRIA is often called "the green heart of Italy." It is a land unto itself, the only region in Italy bordering neither sea nor another country. Umbria is known for its medieval hill towns, dense forests, and local cuisine, particularly foraged truffles and wines.

Umbria is a land particularly suited to viniculture, with a moderate climate and gentle rolling hills that provide exposure to the sun. Since ancient times, Umbrian wine growers have produced excellent wines, and Umbria is particularly known for its white wines, including Pinot Grigio, Trebbiano, Grechetto, Malvasia, and Manzoni Bianco.

Umbria also produces good red wines, from Sangiovese to the more recent introductions—Merlot, Cabernet Sauvignon, and Cabernet Franc.

Of special note, there is also wine made from a grape, Sagrantino, grown only in a very small area of Umbria around Montefalco. The Sagrantino grape has the highest tannic levels of any grape and produces an inky-purple, almost black wine. It was traditionally made in a sweet style, although since the late 1970s, a few winemakers have been producing some dry Sagrantino as well. Because of the extremely high tannin levels, this wine must age for at least ten years to be approachable. I understand it is quite a wonderful wine when it reaches maturity, but since I'm not generally a fan of big, tannic, masculine wines, which are relatively expensive and hard to find because of the limited production, I did not sample any Sagrantino while in Italy. Maybe next time...

# White Blend
# Off the Beaten Track with Cara — Inspired by
# Cirulli Hedone Bianco

**STORY:** Ah, Cara…you probably have a friend like her. You know, the one who always looks like a million bucks, has her own unique style, and turns heads wherever she goes. The one who has an uncanny knack for picking penny stocks, has a source in the cruise industry who gets her bargain prices on first-class cabins, and who always finds an out-of-the-way boutique in Rome or Mendocino and comes home with one-of-a-kind, to-die-for clothes, purchased at department-store prices.

In a city of great restaurants, and overpriced restaurants, she knows the great but value-priced restaurants, often hidden away in unlikely locations. I remember a road trip up the coast with Cara about two years ago. She took the right turn instead of the left I was expecting, taking us winding down narrow back roads and into a small town I'd never heard of. There, we had some of the best food I'd ever eaten, in a small café, served by the owner-chef, with sunset-lit mountains as a backdrop. The price seemed ridiculously low…how did she find this place, I wondered?

Lest you think I'm exaggerating, let me tell you what happened when she came to Italy for a visit. After a few days in Rome, she headed east, over the Apennines, into Umbria.

"Umbria? Not Tuscany?" I asked. "Not the Amalfi Coast?"

"No," she said, "Umbria!" She then ticked off a list of reasons. "Wild, beautiful scenery and national parks, medieval hill towns, few tourists—and of course, great food and wine to be discovered. So many quaint family-run trattorias, so many small family wineries, making great wine as they have for hundreds of years."

After her adventures in Umbria, she came to visit me in Florence, and of course she brought wine from Umbria with her to share.

"I love a winemaker who pours wine all over the rule book," she says. (She would, wouldn't she?) "And who produces a wine *better* than the rules would allow…"

She's pouring me some wine as she speaks. I admire it in my glass—a soft, pale yellow with hints of green. The nose is delicate, almost ethereal, floral, peach and banana. I take a sip, trying to place it. Not quite a Frascati, the signature wine of Rome. Reminiscent of, but no, not the popular Orvieto, from southwestern Umbria. There's something *different* about this wine, *deliciously different*.

"What is it?" I wonder.

"It's lovely, isn't it?" she asks. "I discovered this at a beautiful winery, outside a little village about ten miles north of Orvieto."

I nod, smiling, and savor another mouthful. That's my friend Cara, stumbling onto hidden treasures.

"It's aptly named, don't you think?" She turns the bottle so I can read the label. "Hedone—after the Greek goddess or spirit of pleasure, enjoyment, and delight.

"And amazingly," she continues, "the winemaker says there is an importer back home who can get me a few cases there, so I don't have to ship it myself. I'll bet you can find it here in Florence if you look hard enough, or just go to Umbria for vacation, visit the vineyard, and come home with a case or two."

I'm looking forward to our dinner, which Cara, an amazing cook, I might add, is helping me prepare. She's working on a Caesar salad; I've got pasta and shrimp and scallops cooking. An evening of pure pleasure, indeed.

Meanwhile, I'm thinking about making a visit to Umbria with Paolo, and I make a mental note about the winery and its location. I can't wait to add a few bottles of this wine to my cellar.

**DESCRIPTION:** This Hedone Bianco from the Cirulli winery is crafted from four grape varietals: Trebbiano, Grechetto, Malvasia, and Manzoni Bianco, in equal measure.

Grechetto contributes fruitiness and weight; Trebbiano is more delicately flavored with floral notes and adds food-friendly acidity; Malvasia gives the wine a citrus aspect; and the Manzoni Bianco (or Incrocio Manzoni) brings elegance, acidity, beautiful balance, good body, and a refined, almost delicate character. Clearly, this is a winning combination, in the hands of an artist.

The grapes are carefully selected, immediately cooled to about fifty degrees Fahrenheit, and softly pressed. The juice is clarified through cold settling and ferments slowly for fifteen to eighteen days. Each varietal is vinified separately, to allow for harvesting at the perfect ripeness, and aged for about six months in stainless steel to preserve all the fresh, fruity, and delicate aromas and flavors of the grapes prior to blending.

Cirulli Hedone Bianco is a wine that is guaranteed to bring pleasure to almost any occasion—from sipping as an aperitif through dinner. It is a white wine for all seasons, not just a "summer sipper." If you are looking for something just a little deliciously different and an out-of-the-ordinary white wine (not "just another" Chardonnay or Sauvignon Blanc or Soave that anyone could find) that won't break the budget and can be enjoyed every day, this is the white wine to choose.

Serve at about fifty degrees Fahrenheit for full flavor. Meant to be enjoyed now.

**TASTING NOTES:** Cirulli Hedone Bianco is most often described as "ethereal," and perhaps that is appropriate for a wine named after the spirit of pleasure. It pours into your glass like sunshine spills onto a meadow—soft, clear yellow, with green highlights.

The aromas are of fresh fruits and white flowers.

The taste is fresh and juicy, delicate and creamy, yet expansive. Peach and banana, an intriguing tropical touch, with hints of different citrus fruits, supported by fine mineral and spicy notes. Refreshing, well-balanced, and crisp, with the clear acidity that is the hallmark of food-friendly Italian wines. Hedone Bianco lingers, as pleasure should, long and lasting on the palate.

**FOOD PAIRING:** Cirulli Hedone Bianco is one Italian white wine that can be enjoyed on its own, as an aperitif, allowing you to appreciate all the lovely nuances of its flavor.

It is also excellent with appetizers and first courses like a seafood antipasto (shrimp, scallops, and calamari dressed with oil and lemon), or a light cream soup. We love it with clam chowder or vichyssoise served with prosciutto as-paragus spirals. It's a nice complement to a Caesar salad or salad Nicoise.

It pairs well with pasta with cheese sauces or pasta with seafood, and it is wonderful with risotto with fresh herbs and saffron threads.

And of course, Hedone Bianco works well with chicken and seafood dishes. It's perfect with simple grilled or sautéed white fish with Provençal or Mediterranean-style sauces, served with grilled vegetables.

# *Red Blends*
# *Improv Italian on a French Classic—Inspired by Cirulli Ginepreta*

**STORY**: "Close your eyes, Paolo, and taste this wine."

"Wait, this isn't an Italian wine, is it?" he asks. "It tastes like a right-bank Bordeaux."

"Oh, yes, it is Italian," says my friend Cara. "I found this wine and winery in Umbria last week. You must visit the next time you are there. I think this Umbrian winemaker has really done some 'jazz improvisation' to create this wine."

Cara has such a knack for finding unique things in out-of-the-way places. I always say that's her "sixth sense."

Over wine and dinner of braised lamb neck, which has been simmering in my kitchen as Paolo and I showed Cara some of our favorite places in Florence, the three of us talk about how it really is a small world. Even as long ago as the 1500s, people traveled across continents, bringing their ideas, their foods, their fashions to a new home. Things we think of today as so typical of one country may really have originated in another and "emigrated." For example, French Renaissance architecture is the style of architecture that was imported to France from Italy during the early sixteenth century. During this same period, Catherine de Medici married Henry of Orleans, who became king of France; Catherine brought such dishes as duck à l'orange and onion soup (which we now think of as "oh so French") with her to the French court.

So perhaps it's only fair that in the 1800s, grapes from Bordeaux would make their way to Italy. Italy, of course, has a long tradition of wine making, using native Italian grapes, and producing great wines. But what artist can refuse trying a new medium? What race-car aficionado wouldn't like to get behind the wheel of a new model and see what it can do in his or her hands? What great cook or chef can resist trying a new ingredient or a new cuisine? Winemakers are no different, it seems.

So what happens when a passionate and brilliant Umbrian winemaker, carrying on the traditions of his family, experiments with some of those grapes from Bordeaux? Grapes planted in a very special vineyard, with the perfect terrior for Merlot and for Cabernet Sauvignon. What inspires him to arrive at this blend, reminiscent of a "right-bank" French Bordeaux? We may never know, but the result is pure artistry in a bottle. "Art is wine; wine is art," Valentino Cirulli told Cara on her visit to his winery. He is, of course, right.

So be adventurous, like Cara. We encourage you. Go ahead, break with tradition, and impress your friends and family with braised lamb neck (the "new osso buco" according to our favorite star chef) and this wonderful Italian interpretation of a classic Merlot—Cabernet Sauvignon Bordeaux.

**DESCRIPTION:** If you like French Bordeaux, particularly from those from the right bank, like a Pomerol or a St. Emilion, you should try this Cirulli Ginepreta. Like those, Merlot predominates in this blend.

Cirulli Ginepreta is an intensely fragrant deep ruby-red wine, complex, elegant, and harmonious. The wine takes its name from the vineyard where the Merlot and Cabernet Sauvignon grapes are grown, near the small town of Ficulle in southwestern Umbria. These vineyards have been in the Cirulli family for over 150 years. Generations of experience and love for the land combine with innovation and a passion for excellence to produce this award-winning wine, a beautiful Italian interpretation of a French classic.

This small boutique winery, once known only to a few, won an Oscar in 2010 for this wine. A wine Oscar, that is, at the "Oscar del Vino" held in Rome. Cirulli Ginepreta was selected as "Best Value for the Price." The following year, in 2011, at one of the world's largest wine events, VinItaly, held in Verona, Ginepreta won a Special Mention Award, from among some four thousand exhibitors.

Cirulli Ginepreta is a blend of 85 percent Merlot and 15 percent Cabernet Sauvignon. The varietals are vinified separately, allowing each grape to be harvested at the perfect moment. The wine is aged in oak barriques for twelve months, and then an additional six months in the bottle. The result is a fine, powerful wine, fruity, well structured, and brimming with charm that makes every single glass a treat for your taste buds.

Ginepreta can be enjoyed now, and you can also cellar some bottles to age for another three to perhaps ten years.

Serve at about sixty-four degrees Fahrenheit; open, decant, and allow to breathe and oxygenate for at least an hour to allow the full flavors to evolve.

*TASTING NOTES:* This dark ruby-red wine is intensely fragrant. Blackberry, dark cherry, and red-currant aromas mix harmoniously with chocolate, sweet tobacco, and balsamic notes of rosemary, juniper berries, and licorice.

Ginepreta is an elegant and complex wine, almost voluptuous on the palate. Full flavored and well structured, you will taste notes of jam, spices, licorice, and red fruits, with hints of dried fruits and herbal notes. The tannins are soft, the finish long and persistent.

*FOOD PAIRINGS:* Cirulli Ginepreta is an excellent complement to mature and full-flavored cheeses.

We love it with a variety of risottos—for example, black truffle risotto, or red wine and pork sausage risotto.

For a meal that will transport you to Umbria, try this wine with osso buco, or with braised lamb neck (it's delectable!), braised rabbit with root vegetables, or wild game such as venison or braised wild boar with potatoes.

We also like this wine with roast turkey legs, preferably cooked at a low temperature for a long time, so it falls juicy off the bones.

It also works well with almost any savory dish, dishes redolent of garlic, and of course red meats and tomato-based dishes and sauces.

# *One of a Kind—Inspired by Cirulli 1861 San Valentino*

**STORY:** Have you met him? The consummate Renaissance gentleman. Unconventional. Engaging. Incredible savoir faire.

As much at home in a tux or three-piece suit at a gallery opening as he is in a wool shirt and jeans at a primitive wilderness campsite after hiking a good ten miles…

Writes poetry with a fountain pen, enjoying the sensuous feel of the broad, flexible nib and wet ink gliding across the page. Works at CalTech's Jet Propulsion Lab primarily on NASA projects—serious robotics and software-engineering stuff.

Never follows the crowd. Is as likely to be spending a couple weeks on an archeological project in Ometepe, Nicaragua, as skiing in the Apennines in Umbria or the Dolomites at Val Gardena.

Appreciates the finer things in life. Just look at the lady on his arm, the art on his walls, or his wine cellar.

Should you be lucky enough to be invited for a small, intimate party in his penthouse, you might find the paintings and sculptures stunning, though created by little-known artists. The wine he serves, elegant and impressive, is always from small boutique wineries, purchased at the winery or from a sole importer, never available "mass market."

How I met him and happened to be there at that dinner party, well, that's another story for another time.

On that particular evening, he served a luscious red wine from Umbria. I remember it like it was yesterday. It was a Bordeaux-style wine, primarily Cabernet Franc with a small percentage of Merlot. Almost reminiscent of the famous Chateau Cheval Blanc St. Emilion Grand Cru.

"It takes a special vintner, an artist," he said, "to craft a wine like this. Cabernet Franc is a difficult and demanding grape; the terroir must be right; the care must be right. But when it all comes together, taste the results—an incredible wine, perfumed and seductive." He winked at his lady. She blushed demurely.

He continued, swirling the wine in his glass. "I'm not surprised this Cirulli 1861 San Valentino 2008 won 'Best of Show' in a blind taste testing at the 2012 Wine and Spirits Wholesalers of America (WSWA) Convention and Exposition." He sighed. "But now everyone will want some in their cellar." He, of course, wouldn't tell us where he got his.

Now, fast-forward to me, here in Italy, and my friend Cara's visit. Thanks to her Umbrian adventures, now I too know where to acquire Cirulli 1861 San Valentino wine.

**DESCRIPTION:** This 1861 San Valentino is the flagship wine of Cirulli. It is named in honor of the ancestors of the present owner and vintner, Valentino Cirulli, who began making wine on this land in 1861, the year of the unification of Italy. The vineyards occupy southwest-facing hillsides in southwest Umbria, an ideal location for growing wine grapes.

1861 San Valentino is a warm and intense red wine, 85 percent Cabernet Franc and 15 percent Merlot. The blend and style is reminiscent of right-bank Bordeaux wines, such as the famous Chateau Cheval Blanc St. Emilion Grand Cru—sweeping, intense, suitable for long aging.

The grapes for this wine are carefully selected and immediately cooled to about fifty-five degrees Fahrenheit, followed by maceration in eight-thousand-liter barrels for fifteen to eighteen days. The malolactic fermentation is conducted in barrique, where the wine ages for fifteen to eighteen months. The wine is released for sale only after an additional period of eight to ten months in the bottle.

Cirulli 1861 San Valentino can stand on its own against Napa Valley and French Bordeaux wines that go for twice the price, as evidenced by winning the blind tasting "Best in Show" at the April 2012 Wine & Spirits Wholesalers of America (WSWA) Sixty-Ninth Annual Convention & Exposition held in Las Vegas. It continues to win awards.

Enjoy a bottle now, but definitely tuck a few away to enjoy over the next ten years.

Serve at sixty-four to sixty-eight degrees Fahrenheit. Open and decant for at least an hour to let the full flavor of the wine develop.

**TASTING NOTES:** This is a wine to be savored and appreciated. It glows an intense red in the glass, showing warm ruby reflections—a fine gem.

Swirl, and bring the glass to your nose. This great red wine gives off a fireworks explosion of aromas—ripe red fruits, plums and mulberry, followed by chocolate and anise, then balsamic notes with vanilla and mint from its barrique aging.

On the palate, 1861 San Valentino is intense, warm, and juicy—almost chewable. The oak flavors are well integrated, with dense notes of mint and vanilla complementing the red fruit. The tannins are velvety. Exceptionally well-balanced, this is a true masterpiece of the vintner's art.

**FOOD PAIRINGS:** Cirulli 1861 San Valentino pairs well with a wide variety of foods.

We especially like it with roast leg of lamb with a cherry and red-wine balsamic reduction sauce, and baked or braised fennel. It is also delectable with braised lamb with truffles and wonderful with the best filet mignon or a chateaubriand.

For some classy comfort food fit for an elegant dinner, may I recommend osso buco or braised lamb neck?

Vegetarian? Try this with a torta di spinaci e ricotta, or stuffed portabello mushrooms.

Italians would also pair this with strong cheeses and wild game, especially roast wild boar. (No wild boar in your area? Try roast pork instead.)

1861 San Valentino can also be paired with salmon, perhaps grilled with a bourbon-and-maple marinade and glaze.

# A Rose by Any Other Name—Inspired by Cirulli Hedone Rosso

**STORY:** Paolo and I are finally visiting the Cirulli winery in northwest Umbria, just north of Orvieto, outside the town of Ficulle. We're talking with the owner and vintner, Valentino Cirulli, over a bottle of Cirulli Hedone Rosso.

Ah, what's in a name? As Shakespeare said, "A rose by any other name would smell as sweet." And certainly, this wine would certainly taste as wonderful no matter the name on the label.

But then again, we decide, when a name describes something so perfectly, perhaps there is something in "a name."

Consider:

Hedone: In the philosophy of Epicurus, the great Greek philosopher, hēdonē was the quest for pleasure that would have only good consequences. And Hedone was the name the Greeks gave to the goddess or spirit of pleasure, enjoyment, and delight. Think "hedonistic."

Rosso: Red—the color of this wine.

Cirulli: the family name of the vintner and the winery. The land has been owned by this family since 1860, and the family has been making wine, exceptional wine, for over 150 years. The present Cirulli generation, Valentino, the owner and vintner, expresses his philosophy in the words on the label, "The pleasures of the wine and of the nature that surrounds us." Visit the winery, and you will feel and understand his passion and commitment, and his love for the land and creating exceptional wines.

Tasting this red wine, Hedone Rosso, we tell Valentino that we think perhaps the name is perfect and could be nothing else. It is a pure delight to drink. It epitomizes the magic a good vintner works, creating from the pleasure of the harvest—the fruit of the good earth of Umbria, the sun, and the rain—the pleasure of a great wine, easy to drink, the perfect accompaniment a wide variety of food. Something to bring "Hedone" to your table any day and every day.

Paolo and I add several bottles to our collection. After all, we too appreciate "hēdonē."

**DESCRIPTION:** Paolo and I have decided that the best description of this Cirulle Hedone Rosso, other than pure pleasure in a glass, is perhaps " a Super Umbrian"—like a Super Tuscan, but unoaked and more affordable. This is a wine you can afford to kick back with at the end of the day, or crack open at a moment's notice when friends drop over, and thoroughly enjoy.

It's an inspired blend of Sangiovese and the trio from Bordeaux— Merlot, Cabernet Franc, and Cabernet Sauvignon. The varietals are vinified separately, aged about six months in stainless steel, and then blended to achieve the vintner's vision for a high-quality red wine that you can enjoy every day. The result is a fruity, complex, and rich wine, elegant and velvety.

Serve at sixty to sixty-five degrees Fahrenheit.

**TASTING NOTES:** Bright red, with overtones of violet, Hedone Rosso pours into your glass like liquid rubies.

Swirl, close your eyes, and inhale. It's a complex, many-layered fruity bouquet, reflecting the skill of the winemaker and the echoes of each of four grapes that are so perfectly blended—plums, red cherries, cassis (the liqueur from black currants), with deeper hints of prune, perhaps.

The taste is elegant and rich, powerful and complex on the palate, yet fresh and fruity. It's a velvety blend of those fruits on the nose—red cherries, plums, black and red currants. It has a soft, lingering finish. This is a wine of great complexity and richness.

**FOOD PAIRINGS:** Hedone Rosso is an elegant and versatile red wine that pairs well with both white and red meats. The perfect solution when you want to bring a wine but don't know if your hostess is serving chicken or beef.

We love its soft, velvety, and fruity taste with fresh or slightly mature soft cheeses—try it with a brie or camembert. For something elegant, pair this with a baked brie—we like it with phyllo-wrapped brie with apricot and rosemary chutney, or brie baked with caramelized onions or pears.

It's light and elegant enough to pair with many light summer dishes, yet complex and structured enough to work well with lamb or even barbeque. We also enjoy it with duck.

Vegetarians will love it with vegetable gratins and a wide range of risottos.

# Pinot Grigio
## All That Jazz—Inspired by Ganzo Pinot Grigio

Probably the most popular imported wine in America, and thought of as
"The Italian white."

**STORY:** Paolo and I find his cousin Francesca at a table in the Piazza IV
Novembre, ravishing as always, in a white and bright golden-yellow sundress,
and wearing a face-shading straw hat and dark glasses. It's her "movie star"
look, and perfect for the day.

It's early July and hot here in Perugia, the capital of the region of Umbria.
But Francesca, she's looking cool. Maybe being a native helps. Or perhaps it's
the cold white wine she's sipping from the glass poised elegantly in her hand.
The bright-yellow label on the chilled bottle of Pinot Grigio matches her dress
and the ribbon in her hat. Aahhh, Francesca, what a perfect picture.

Umbria is known for its verdant beauty, its lakes, and the breathtaking
540–foot-tall Marmore Falls, which Paolo and I visited on our way to Perugia.
The falls were created in 270 BC by the Romans, when they dug a canal
from a mosquito-infested swamp to a cliff high above the Nera River. Of
course, Umbria also has wonderful wine and food, and picturesque medieval
hill towns with beautiful churches. Perugia, as famous for its chocolate as
its churches, is one of those lovely old towns. Both Umbria and Perugia are
world-famous for the Umbria Jazz Festival, which has been held here since
1973. And the Umbria Jazz Festival is the reason Paolo and I are in Perugia.
Attending is a tradition with Francesca and Paolo, who are jazz aficionados,
and this year, I'm with Paolo.

The Festival hosts some of the greatest names in jazz, from all over the
world, as well as wonderful new talent. In the past, artists like Miles Davis,
Dizzy Gillespie, Herbie Hancock, Miles Shorter, Santana, B. B. King, Sting,
Gilberto Gil, Sergio Mendes, Chick Corea, and Pat Metheny have all per-
formed here.

There is music everywhere, for everyone. Gospel music spilling from an ancient church will lure you into the cool darkness. Around another corner, an enthusiastic crowd is following a marching band that came all the way from New Orleans down Corso Vannucci, past the historic palaces and churches and street cafés with jazz aficionados and locals sipping wine or espresso. Every piazza seems to host a jam session or performance. In the eighteenth-century Morlacchi Theatre, in small clubs located in the cellars of medieval palaces, and in the National Gallery of Umbria, containing one of Italy's most important collections of medieval and Renaissance art, the concerts and jam sessions go on until dawn.

It's the first day of the festival, and Francesca and Paolo always attend at least one of the two "Bottega del Vino" events—Jazz, Wine & Gourmet Cuisine at 1:00 p.m. or Wine Aperitif & Dinner & Jazz starting at 7:00 p.m. These almost always feature Italian jazz musicians.

It's just before one o'clock when Paolo and I settle into our seats at the table with Francesca. The music begins; lunch is ordered. The wine Fracesca has selected this year is a gem and a perfect match, not only for Francesca's outfit, as I mentioned earlier, but also for the occassion—Ganzo Pinot Grigio. It may be a hot summer afternoon, but the jazz is ganzo—"cool" in Italian—as is this wine. Fresh, crisp, easy to drink as an aperitif, and perfect with the grilled chicken we've just ordered. Life doesn't get much better than this!

**DESCRIPTION:** Ganzo Pinot Grigio is a classic Italian Pinot Grigio, crafted in Umbria. There may be wine snobs who scorn Pinot Grigio, but there are some truly admirable Pinot Grigios, like this one. And while Pinot Grigio has many aficionados here in Europe, it's probably the most popular imported wine in America.

Italian Pinot Grigio has a reputation as an easy-to-drink summertime wine—a perfect aperitif for sipping while listening to jazz, for example, or with light summer fare. Generally Pinot Grigios don't require a lot of thought, since they're light and refreshing, and frankly, when it's hot, who has the energy for cogitating? Serve nicely chilled, put on some music, and make your summer afternoon "ganzo"!

**TASTING NOTES:** Everything about this wine says "refreshing." The color is a luminous light straw yellow, with the slightest hints of pale green as it's poured into the glass. The nose is soft, reminiscent of pears and apples, hints of soft summer flowers, and a breeze off the lake. The taste of this Ganzo Pinot Grigio is truly refreshing—very clean and crisp, yet elegant. It's fresh and slightly fruity, with notes of apple, citrus, and hints of honey, that combine with an elegant acidity and attractive minerality on the palate.

**FOOD PAIRINGS:** Ganzo Pinot Grigio is an excellent aperitif wine. It also matches well with dishes from various climates and cultures: from sushi to rich salads, curry and omelettes, pasta, and risotto with seafood.

For appetizer pairing, it blends nicely with pecorino—a sheep's milk cheese that has been made in Umbria and neighboring Tuscany for thousands of years.

We like it with clam soup (*zuppa di vongole*), goat cheese with rocket salad, deep-fried calamari salad, green-lipped mussels, or simply grilled fish or chicken.

For a memorable combination, try it with cold barbecued chicken basted in a moderately spicy Thai sauce.

# Region: Abruzzo

**Wines:**
Montepulciano d'Abruzzo
Cerasuolo d'Abruzzo
Trebbaino d'Abruzzo
Pecorino

**Wineries:**
L'Artiste
La Valentina
Estate Tiberio

# Abruzzo

———— ❦ ————

DUE EAST FROM Rome lies the region of Abruzzo, stretching from the Apennines, with skiing comparable to the Alps, to the Adriatic coast with beautiful beaches.

One of Italy's most beautiful regions, Abruzzo features what are arguably the most picturesque landscapes of central Italy outside of Tuscany, although it is often overlooked by tourists, for which I am thankful. It has spectacular natural scenery, medieval castles and villages, monasteries, and Roman ruins. Two-thirds of Abruzzo's land is mountainous, with the rest being hills and coast. A third of the region is designated as national or regional parkland.

The long coastline hugging the Adriatic Sea and the mountainous interior also provide myriad of microclimates and terroirs. It's a land of vineyards and olive groves. The Abruzzi area has been noted in history for its viniculture as far back as the seventh century BC. Throughout history, noted poets and storytellers, including Ovid, who lived in Abruzzo, have been inspired by and written about the wines of Abruzzo.

"It warms the blood, adds luster to the eyes,
And wine and love have ever been allies."
—Ovid

The climate in the region is heavily influenced by the Apennine mountain range that runs north-south down Italy's middle; Abruzzo's Gran Sasso massif, at 2,914 meters (9,560 feet) above sea level, is the highest point in the range. It follows that the region's interior has a continental climate, with frigid, snowy winters and cooler summers, while the coastline is characterized by a temperate Mediterranean climate. The geology is also highly varied, with marly-clay, sand-rich flysch, and limestone soils. Gravels and alluvial deposits dominate the coastline's flatland viticultural areas. For all these reasons, Abruzzo's wines offer noteworthy differences, even when they're made from the same grape variety.

Historically a poor region whose people were shepherds and farmers, their descendants are proud and independent, and incredibly friendly. The food and wine might be considered rustic, *"cucina povera"* (peasant food), reflecting this heritage, but it is also fresh, delicious, and served in generous portions.

The region also offers sybarites a bounty of high-quality food products, including saffron (Italy's finest), white and black truffles, porcini and vegetables, flavorful fish and crustaceans, unique pasta dishes, Italy's best lamb, and local cheeses and salumi too numerous to count.

Abruzzo might well be called a region for all seasons. Skiing in the winter, either downhill or cross-country, where you might be surprised to find your ski tips following the footprints of a bear. Hiking in the other seasons, you could wander through dappled sunlight through beech woods, on pathways past waterfalls and pools, or through verdant meadows filled with fragrant scents, soothing sounds, and hundreds of wildflowers. In the spring, you might be startled from your reverie by a cinghiale (wild boar) or a deer. Lazing on a sun-drenched beach, the turquoise Adriatic stretched out before you, you could be forgiven for thinking you have found paradise. Yes, every season has its own magic in this Italian Eden.

# Montipulcinao d' Abruzzo
# A Wine for All Reasons—Inspired by
# L'Artista Montepulciano d' Abruzzo

Perfect for the wine lover on a budget—Montepulciano d'Abruzzo is a lively, well-balanced red wine from Abruzzi, versatile as Barbera or Beaujolais.

**STORY:** Paolo is an avid skier. I am not. I tried skiing once, several years ago, even taking some lessons, but after enduring three painful hours just to get down a beginner's slope, with falls too numerous to count, I retired to the lodge. As I sat in front of the fireplace, nursing my sore muscles and bruises and with a stiff drink in hand, I concluded that, at least for me, skiing was "the agony of de fall, and the thrill of defrost." So, I send Paolo off for a skiing holiday in the Apennines, in Abruzzo.

He returns happily, with stories to share, and wine from Abruzzo. Sitting in front of the fire, with glasses of Montepulciano d'Abruzzo in hand, our appetites sated with *bucatini alla trescatora*, an Abruzzo pasta dish made with duck that Paolo has recreated, I think I got the best end of the deal—Abruzzo wine and food, Paolo and I in front of a fire, and no skiing to contend with in person. I felt rather blessed to be able to live vicariously through the magic of Paolo's vivid and enthusiastic descriptions of his skiing escapades, virtual skiing without the pain.

"It's some of the best skiing outside the Alps," Paolo says. "Some areas often have more snow than the Alps do. Roccaraso, the oldest and still the premier ski area in Abruzzo, where I stayed, is one of those. There are runs there starting at over sixty-five hundred feet, and from some of these, I could see the blue Adriatic in the distance."

I tell him, only half-jokingly, I'd rather be dipping my toes in the Adriatic than in the snow. He promises me a trip to enjoy both the wild mountain scenery and the seacoast in warmer weather. Ah, I'm such a lucky girl.

Paolo continues, clearly relishing reliving his skiing adventure. "This trip, I saw a pair of golden eagles. I've been fortunate, in other years, skiing in different areas, to see bear, Apennine wolves, and once, the rare Abruzzo chamois. I think that was in either the Abruzzo National Park, near Pescasseroli, or Campo Imperatore, in the Gran Sasso National Park, known as Italy's 'Little Tibet.' We should visit there for hiking.

"After a day of skiing the uncrowded Abruzzi slopes, I'd sit back in front of a fire, in a charming medieval town, reliving each run with good friends, some great food, and a bottle of this local red wine, Montepulciano d'Abruzzo. The only thing that could have made it better would have been to have you there.

"Did you know that if you had been a soldier in Hannibal's army, over two millennia ago, you would have been revived after your arduous march across the Alps and your battles to defeat the Romans by wine made from these Montepulciano grapes in Abruzzo?" Paolo asks. Then, not waiting for a response, he adds, "And I've read several chronicles of the Punic Wars that mention this wine specifically, citing both its excellence and its restorative powers, for both man and horse! I found it very restorative myself, the perfect wine after a long day of skiing."

Paolo continues to rave about the restorative powers of the Abruzzo wines he enjoyed on his skiing vacation, and elaborates in great detail on the wine, the food, and the scenery he so passionately enjoyed. He speaks with such excitement and enthusiasm that I feel I was there with him, and in all respects except for the skiing, I fervently wish I had been.

Several months later, Paolo and I travel the road from Rome east to the Abruzzi seacoast town of Pescara, passing over the spine of the Apennines, and then through the Peligna valley. Gran Sasso National Park and Campo Imperatore lie to the north, Pescassaroli and the Abruzzi National Park to the south. The fertile valley, an ancient lakebed, is famous for its agriculture, including, of course, its vineyards, and especially the Montepulciano wines.

We spend some time in the mountains hiking on trails through forests and wildflower-filled meadows, past waterfalls and stone shepherd's huts, up steep rocky escarpments, to what feels like the top of the world, as mountains, hillsides, valleys, and ancient towns, clinging to cliffs and perched on hilltops, spread out before us.

We hike up to one of Europe's highest ancient fortresses, Rocca Calascio, now a ruin, which looks vaguely familiar to me. "Ah, yes, it should," says Paolo, as we set out our modest picnic lunch of local-made salami and cheese we picked up in the village butcher shop, rustic bread from the bakery, and of course a bottle of the local Montepulciano, one with a beautiful label reflecting its name, *L'Artista*. "Rocco Calascio is a favorite of filmmakers. This place has been the setting for over twenty movies, including *Krull, The Name of the Rose,* and *Ladyhawke*."

Paolo and I first had L'Artista Montepulciano d'Abruzzo back in Florence, when we were at a gallery opening for one of our favorite young artists in Florence, Stefano Ramunno. Not only did he create the label, but he said it was his favorite red wine. Stephano described it as "a lovely work of traditional wine-making art, capturing all the beauty and poetry of Abruzzo in a bottle. And, its price allows even a young struggliing artist to enjoy it with every meal." Ever the artist, he continued, "It embraces and enhances a good meal much as a good illustration adds to a story." This analogy was perfect; I immediately thought of Beatrice Potter's *Peter Rabbit*, and Maurice Sendak's *Where the Wild Things Are.* We were delighted to find it here, to accompany our lunch.

Later in the day, in another village down in the Peligna Valley, we enjoy one of the most traditional of Abruzzi dishes, *arrosticini* (chunks of lamb, grilled over coals, that seem to melt in your mouth) served simply with bread, olive oil, peperoncini, and of course, according to tradition, a bottle of Montepulciano d'Abruzzo. We found ourselves talking with the local doctor, who grew up in this area.

"Ah," he says, nodding at me, "you are American. So you probably know that red wine has been shown, in over a dozen studies by medical schools and even your National Institutes of Health, to contain heart-healthy compounds such as antioxidants, antocyans, and polyphenols like resveratrol."

I nod yes, although maybe I didn't remember the exact names of those "healthy compounds." I remember thinking when I learned this fact, "Another good reason to drink wine!"

"But did you know," he continues, "that recent studies have shown that Montepulciano wine has some of the highest levels of these compounds of any red wine? Perhaps this accounts for the high number of centenarians, and active eighty- and ninety-year-olds, found in the small villages in this valley, who of course have been drinking their local Montepulciano wines all their long lives."

We raise a toast to good wine, good health, and long life.

So many reasons to enjoy this Montepulciano d'Abruzzo wine: it's healthy; it's restorative; it's delicious and easy to drink; it goes well with almost any food, embracing and enhancing it; it's been enjoyed by warriors (Hannibal) and nobility (the Medicis) and simple folk (shepherds and farmers) down through history; and it's a great value—simple and uncomplicated perfection. We brought a case of L'Artista Montepulciano d'Abruzzo home with us as a reminder of our trip.

*DESCRIPTION:* A bit of clarification and to dispel any confusion—yes, there is a town in Tuscany that bears the name of Montepulciano. And yes, there is a wine produced there that bears the name of the town—*Vino Nobile di Montepulciano.* The name of this wine, *Montepulciano D'Abruzzo*, refers to the name of the variety of grape used to make the wine.

Montepulciano d'Abruzzo is perhaps one of the most authentic expressions of the Italian wine tradition. With a few exceptions, the Montepulciano grape is still vinified following traditional simple methods. The wine produced is usually robust, rustic, with a lot of minerality, and at the same time rich and complex. It has been called "the perfect food wine." And while these Abruzzo reds can be enjoyed young, *"vino novella"*—similar to a Beaujolais Nouveau—they also have good ageing potential, although most will not change significantly, even after ten or more years in the cellar. Remarkably, given all these stellar qualities, they are still very affordable. Perhaps all of this would explain why Montepulciano d'Abruzzo is one of the most popular red wines in Italy today.

Serve at sixty to sixty-five degrees Fahrenheit; open and allow to breathe for about an hour to savor its full luscious and smooth flavors.

**TASTING NOTES:** This is *not* "just another red wine." It may be classified as "rustic," or perhaps better described as "miscast" as a simple peasant wine. It is rather, in my mind, a wine of jewels—the color of the finest rubies, and velvety smooth, well-balanced, subtly complex and structured—fruity and spicy, with soft tannins, good acidity, and a nice minerality.

Swirl it in your glass—dark, deep rubies and garnets glow in the firelight. It's an aromatic red wine, fruity and fragrant, conjuring up lost memories of childhood, picking blackberries and raspberries, and Granny's sweet-sour plum crumble cooling on the kitchen window ledge. A sip confirms this—it's a juicy mouthful of ripe blackberries and black cherries, a twist of damson acidity, an adult sprinkling of spice and anise, and perhaps a hint of dark chocolate. The finish is clean and persistent.

**FOOD PAIRINGS:** If you are looking for "the perfect food wine" that literally is good to drink with just about everything, this is your wine. Not sure what wine to bring to a dinner party, a picnic, or any type of get-together? This Montepulciano d'Abruzzo solves your problem. It's a brilliant party wine, and we have yet to find food we cannot enjoy this with. Perhaps that is partly because of the cuisine of Abruzzo that it is made for—it has to compete against the fiery Abruzzo pepperoncino chili, so rather than fight a dish, it embraces it.

If your dinner table features simple pasta dishes, antipasto plates, salads, and rustic artisanal breads, L'Artista Montepulciano D'Abruzzo pairs perfectly with casual, everyday Italian cuisine. Try one of the signature pasta dishes of Abruzzo, *bucatini alla trescatora*, which Paolo made for me that winter evening to share his skiing trip with me. Cut a duck into pieces. If there is a lot of fat under the skin, score the skin. Fry over medium heat, turning often, so the fat releases and the duck skin turns a nice golden color. Remove the duck and the extra duck fat (save it for frying potatoes another day!). Add chopped onions, celery, and carrot to the pan, and cook until limp, partially cooked, and golden. Deglaze the pan with white wine. Add the duck back into the pan. Cook about thirty minutes. Add a can of crushed or diced tomatoes and some tomato paste, a little marjoram, and a sprinkle of nutmeg, stir, and cook another thirty minutes. Cook pasta until al dente, drain, put in a dish, stir the duck sauce over the pasta, and place the duck pieces on top to serve. Add some good bread and a salad, maybe with some of those pepperoncini on the side, and you're in Abruzzo.

And remember that arrosticino? Grilled lamb kebabs by another name? This Montepulciano d'Abruzzo is the perfect mate for lamb. In fact, it's perfect for any Sunday afternoon cookout or any tailgate party—whether you're grilling up burgers and chili dogs, barbequed ribs or chicken, grilled salmon, or big juicy steaks. It is perfect with these rich, marbled meats because it provides rich, fruity notes together with zesty acids to balance all the fat.

And yes, it's wonderful with any meat-lover's pizza, especially sausage and peperoni.

For something different, remembering how well it goes with the spicy cuisine of Abruzzo, try it with tandoori chicken or Caribbean cuisine!

For a bit of "comfort food" on a cold night, try it with earthy soups, including those with lots of beans and legumes, or even a French cassoulet!

# Cerasuolo d' Abruzzo
## Saffron, Chickpeas, and Donkeys? —Inspired by La Valentina Cerasuolo d' Abruzzo

**STORY:** It's the most expensive spice in the world, selling for more than the price of an equivalent weight of gold. It's been treasured by many of history's greatest civilizations, and not just for cooking. Buddhists and Hindus consider it sacred and dye monks' robes with it. Ancient Egyptians used it in medicines and perfumes. Cleopatra considered it an essential scent for seduction. Minoan women on Crete colored their lips and nipples with it. Hippocrates wrote of its medical powers. Romans bathed in it, added it to wine, and perfumed theaters with it. In the Middle Ages, it was used to treat a variety of illnesses and to color illuminated manuscripts. Its name comes from ancient Arabic "zafaran"—"the hair of angels."

Paolo is determined that we shall add some L'Aquila saffron—"Abruzzo's red gold"—to our pantry this year. It is generally agreed by chefs and gourmets alike to be the very best in the world, and Paolo says that I deserve the very best. It is grown only on the Navelli plain in Abruzzo.

The third weekend in August finds us, therefore, in Navelli. This is when the "Sagre dei Ceci and Zafferano" is held—"The Festival of Chickpeas and Saffron."

I arrive in Navelli expecting to see fields of purple crocuses spreading out below the town. The contrast with the golden stone of the buildings and the green of the countryside would be stunning, but instead of purple, the crocus fields are neatly groomed deep brown.

I soon learn the reason for the disparity between what I expected and what I was actually seeing. This festival does correspond to the harvest of the ceci (a local variety of chickpea), which takes place from the end of July through August, and also to the time of the Feast of the Assumption. The saffron bulbs, however, were just planted. They will not be in bloom until sometime in mid-October to mid-November. Since the weather at saffron harvest time is chilly, the exact dates of the harvest cannot be predicted long in advance, and the harvest is an intense and busy time, with no time or energy for festivities—or mass crowds of tourists—the saffron festival is held in conjunction with the chickpea-harvest festival. Fortunately, Paolo can purchase some of last year's saffron crop, which will be for sale during the festival.

Sergio, Paolo's friend and former roommate at university, is joining us. He is originally from Navelli and a regular at the Harvest Festival. We meet him for lunch in a small, unassuming restaurant, "The Crocus." However, it is run by a relative of Sergio's, and we are pretty sure the food will be great. We aren't disappointed. Sergio orders a light antipasti platter with prosciutto-wrapped melon, pepperoncini, and some cheese, a saffron-and-sausage pizza and pasta e ceci for us.

Sergio pairs our lunch dishes with a rosato wine—Cerasuolo d' Abruzzo, from a small winery, La Valentina, not far from the seaside town of Pescara. "Taste the fruit and the sea breeze," says Sergio. The waiter brings the bottle of nicely chilled, gorgeous cherry-red wine to the table. I swirl and sip—it's lovely, and I know it will complement everything we are having.

The pizza is amazing—who would have thought of saffron on pizza with sausage?

Sergio says, "The pasta e ceci is not quite as good as my grandmother's, but since she's no longer here to make it for me, I think this is a good substitute."

I'd never had this before, but it's sort of like a cousin to *pasta e fagiole*, only somehow more satisfying. It's midway between a soup and pasta with sauce. I imagine making this in the winter as an antidote to a chill, blustery day. The ceci are much smaller than the chickpeas I'm familiar with, very creamy, and with a delicious nuttiness.

After lunch, we wander the streets of Navelli. Paolo selects small vials of saffron from several vendors, and bags of dried ceci as well. The scent of the saffron is intriguing—dark, sweet, a little musky and earthy. "I'll make you Risotto alla Milanese to die for," says Paolo, pressing his fingers to his lips with a kiss and a quick wave, so typically Italian; then he adds, "And saffron custard. And did I tell you saffron is reputed to be an aphrodisiac?" He winks and smiles that devilish smile that never fails to charm me.

About four thirty, Sergio collects us, gets another bottle of Cerasuolo d'Abruzzo, and leads us down the hill from the town to a huge field. A race-track has been marked off. "Welcome to the Navelli Palio," Sergio proudly announces.

I'm familiar with the famous Palio in Siena, where ten Italian-bred horses race around the tight corners and narrow track set up in the Piazza del Campo. It's an ancient tradition—depending on whom you ask, dating back to sometime between 1633 and 1701. The horses and jockeys each represent one of the city guilds. The jockeys wear colorful costumes denoting their guild, and they ride bareback. It's the most amazing ninety-second horse race you will ever see.

"This is a little different kind of Palio," says Sergio. "I was honored to be selected as a jockey when I was a young teenager. There are eight racers, and each represents a different district in the city.

"See, here they come now," Sergio says excitedly, pointing to the top of the hill. From my vantage point, this appears to be a medieval parade, featuring a good portion of the town dressed in colorful medieval costume. First is a brass band, followed by the "cecetti and cecette"—local children, brightly dressed, the horde named after the local petite chickpeas, clearly a term of endearment. Next come young men and women, each pair attired in tunics and tights, like medieval pages or squires might have worn, each pair reflecting the colors and pattern of the district they represent. They are leading donkeys draped with blankets like medieval chargers might have worn, and that, to the bemusement of onlookers, are somewhat less than cooperative about making their way down the hill.

Sergio explains, "Unlike the Palio in Siena, where horses and riders train for months for the race, these donkeys have just been pulled from farmer's fields and are, for the most part, totally untrained. The riders and the young ladies who are the donkey leaders haven't practiced the art of donkey riding and leading, either." He chuckles. "It makes for a much more interesting and entertaining race."

Watching the volunteer lady "squires" trying to get the eight donkeys lined up at the starting line, with jockeys astride them, is quite a show. Some of the donkeys are a bit frisky; others, clearly males, are trying to take advantage of their close proximity to female donkeys and engage in a little mating activity before the race. This of course solicits embarrassed gasps and raucous hoots from the crowd.

Eventually, the "squires" get the mounts under control, noses at the starting line, and jockeys all on board, at least for the moment. They're off! Or sort of. The jockeys attempt to stay on and ride their donkeys, as the lady squires do everything they can to get those stubborn asses around the course, not once, but four times! They pull; they push. The jockeys get off and try to help, especially when the donkey decides to canter off in the wrong direction, dragging the squire along. It's chaos; it's mayhem; it's hilarious! I struggle not to pee in my panties, I'm laughing so hard. Finally, it's over, and with the winner declared, we raise a toast with our Cerasuolo d'Abruzzo.

Ever since that most memorable experience, whenever I open a bottle of Cerasuolo d'Abruzzo, I don't know whether to laugh or sigh, depending on which memory surfaces first—the memory of the Palio degli Asini, or of Paolo's Risotto alla Milanese and saffron custard.

**DESCRIPTION:** Cerasuolo 'd Abruzzo has been called Italy's best rosato—rosé—wine, and this La Valentina Cerasuolo is certainly a great example. Cerasuolo d'Abruzzo is darker in color than most rosés, and a bit more assertive in flavor. The attractive cherry-red color gives the wine its name: cerasuolo means "cherry" in Italian. It's made from Montepulciano d'Abruzzo grapes, using the maceration method. The red grapes are pressed, but after a few hours of maceration or fermentation time, the juice is drained off from the skins. La Valentina's winemaker leaves the juice with the skins for about eighteen hours, resulting in the cherry-red color and a bright, fruity bouquet and taste. The wine is fermented in stainless-steel tanks.

***TASTING NOTES:*** La Valentina Cerasuolo d'Abruzzo is a particularly pleasant and charming wine, displaying extraordinary freshness. It is medium-bodied, balanced, and intense, with great persistence.

Swirl and sniff—you'll encounter an elegant fragrance—delicately winey, fruity, fine, and intense. In keeping with its cherry color, you'll detect aromas of red berries (strawberry with a hint of cherry) and also delicate herbs and spice notes.

Then taste. The flavors are dry, soft, harmonious, and even delicate. I detect cranberry, strawberry, and pomegranate jam, with an almond aftertaste.

***FOOD PAIRINGS:*** Of course, Cerasuolo d'Abruzzo is the perfect wine to sip, nicely chilled, on a warm summer day or evening. On the beach, by a pool, on the porch swing, a little music, party for twenty—or, perhaps, just two.

It's perfect with all manner of antipasti and stunning with prosciutto—think prosciutto-wrapped melon or asparagus. Try it with sushi for some cross-cultural culinary greatness!

It complements soups, from summer soups like gazpacho and vichyssoise to winter favorites like pasta e fagioli and pasta e ceci, because it pairs so well with legumes and grains. We love it with a summer peach soup, too.

Of course, it's excellent with lighter pastas, a nice risotto Milanese (made with the saffron Abruzzo is famous for), chicken, and seafood of all types. We find it works exceptionally well in the summer with grilled salmon or tuna steaks.

Try Sergio's grandmother's pasta e ceci with this: Cook chickpeas (ceci if you can find them) with a bay leaf, garlic, rosemary, and chili or red-pepper flakes until the chickpeas are soft and creamy. Remove the bay leaf and rosemary. In another saucepan, heat olive oil, and cook chopped onion until soft and translucent; then add a cup of crushed tomatoes, and heat until slightly thickened. Take a cup of the cooked chickpeas with the clove of garlic they cooked with, and puree in a blender until smooth. Add the blended chick-peas and the tomatoes into the saucepan with the remaining whole cooked chickpeas and their cooking liquid. Add pasta (we like tubetti or garganelli or other smaller, short-cut pasta) and cook until al dente and the sauce has thickened, stirring frequently to keep it from sticking or burning. We keep a little warm chicken stock or tomato juices in reserve to add if needed. This dish is meant to be more "soup-like" than traditional pasta with sauce. Season with course-ground black pepper, a little good olive oil, and parmesan cheese. True Abruzzo comfort food.

# Trebbaino d' Abruzzo
## A Case of Mistaken Identity — Inspired by Estate Tiberio Trebbaino d' Abruzzo

**STORY:** I confess, I was never much of a fan of Trebbaino wine, especially before I came to Italy. I found even the best of them uninspiring and ordinary, barely deserving of the terms "fresh," "citrusy," or "floral." The worst seemed almost tasteless, verging on bitter or sour. If this was your first introduction to "real wine," you would probably be inclined to go back to your Boone's Farm or Pink Moscato.

After arriving in Florence, I occasionally was persuaded to try a Trebbaino. On most of these experimental forays I was unimpressed, but every once in a while I would stumble across an outstanding bottle. When this occurred it was like a jolt of summer lightning, the wine redolent of elderflowers, angelica, and green apples, or citrus and stone fruits, spices and exotic florals. I often wondered why there was such variation; even Paolo, normally a wealth of answers on most things food and wine in Tuscany, had no answers.

This mystery continued for quite some time. The usual explanations of regional variations, terroir, weather, vintner skills and vision, and even grape clones, did not seem sufficient. I read wine labels, hoping to find a clue. I kept notes about those Trebbainos I liked, and those I was less fond of. Still, I was no wiser about why there were such differences.

I finally decided that maybe if I "go to the horse's mouth," I will get some answers. One Trebbaino I have consistently liked, since first sampling it here in Florence, is from a small winery in Abruzzo. It's a Trebbaino d'Abruzzo, from Estate Tiberio. You know how Paolo and I like small wineries, and meeting the owners and winemaker. With Paolo's promised summer trip to Abruzzo coming up, we can plan a stop at the winery, which is near Cugnoli, one of those small (six hundred families in residence), charming medieval hilltop villages, nestled in the foothills of the Apennines, and a mere twenty-three miles from the seacoast. I hear they have a nice restaurant in town as well, with the unlikely name of "Champignon."

I am forever grateful that Paolo and I made the trip. Thanks to Cristiana and Antonio Tiberio, I now consistently choose good Trebbaino wine. I think of them, and that beautiful day in the Estate Tiberio vineyard, whenever I'm enjoying a good glass of Trebbaino d'Abruzzo. I'm sharing this with you so you, too, can discover what a good Trebbaino can taste like.

"The secret," Cristiana says, "is that the wine must be made with Trebbaino Abruzzese grapes. I estimate that less than twenty percent of all Trebbaino d'Abruzzo wine is actually made with Trebbaino Abruzzese grapes. True Trebbiano Abruzzese is rare; many of Abruzzo's vineyards are actually planted to Bombino Bianco, Mostosa, and Trebbiano Toscano, which were, until very recently, routinely confused with Trebbiano Abruzzese. However, while the four share similar features, they are distinct varieties.

"Look carefully," Cristina says, walking along a row of vines separate from the main vineyard. She continues, "There is no way one can confuse Trebbaino Abruzzese with Bombino Bianco, Trebbaino Toscano, or other varieties. If you look closely at the vines and grapes, you will see that they look completely different. If anything, I think it's a Passerina that people most often mistakenly identify as Trebbaino Abruzzese. See here, Trebbaino Abruzzese is characterized by large leaves with five lobes, and large, pyramidal bunches of grapes with medium-large berries that have little bloom. The large leaves protect the berries well from sunlight; the grapes rarely become darker than a deep straw green, even when fully ripe, so unlike other Trebbainos whose berries ripen to a yellow or even reddish gold. This is true even when producers remove leaves to maximize ripening."

I study the vines, which are labeled by variety, and agree. Even I can see some distinct differences.

"In fact," Cristiana continues, "the University of Milan did a DNA study of all seven of the grapes in the Trebbaino family, and also seventeen others that look similar, like Bombino and Passerina, to see how closely they were related." Cristiana chuckles. "The results showed that these Trebbaino 'siblings' were actually all adopted into the Trebbaino family, and not related at all.

"The study authors also thought that the name 'Trebbaino' came from the French word *Draibio*, meaning 'vigorous shoot.' In other words, the name was not intended to identify a particular grape that came from a particular place, but rather to describe a broad category of grapes. The introduction of these vigorous and productive varieties was probably due to the agrarian policy of Charlemagne, who promoted a rapid renewal of medieval Italian viticulture after the fall and breakdown of the Roman Empire."

Cristian completes the puzzle with a little history of the grapes and the vineyard.

"My father, Riccardo Tiberio, was an export manager for a well-known winery here in Abruzzo, and he knew well what truly high-quality Abruzzo grapes could offer and what the modern world expected in wines. In 2000, he found a very old plot of Trebbiano Abruzzese vines, which, despite the variety's name, was a rarity in Abruzzo. He was so excited by his discovery of these sixty-year-old vines that he decided to change his and his family's destiny. So, he purchased the eight-hectare plot of Trebbiano Abruzzese vines he had fallen in love with, along with another thirty-one hectares of land suitable for planting and wine production. These are the vineyards you see today. We released our first vintage in 2004 and have won numerous awards for our wines."

Mystery solved, Paolo and I adjourn, with several bottles of Estate Tiberio Trebbaino d'Abruzzo in hand, to lunch at "Restaurante Champignon." Seems more than grape varieties have a French connection here in Abruzzo.

**DESCRIPTION:** The Estate Tiberio Trebbaino d'Abruzzo is made solely from Trebbaino Abruzzese grapes from that vineyard with the sixty-year-old vines. The vineyard lies some twelve hundred feet above sea level; the soil is limestone, a marly-clay with limestone over a sandstone-rich bedrock. After the harvest at the end of September, the grapes are crushed, but not pressed; just the free-run juice is collected. It is fermented with indigenous yeasts in stainless-steel tanks.

If you cannot find Estate Tiberio Trebbaino d'Abruzzo, and you want a high-quality Trebbaino like theirs, you must be sure the wine you are choosing is a Trebbaino d'Abruzzo and, more importantly, is made with Trebbaino Abruzzese grapes. Not all Trebbaino d'Abruzzo wines are—some are made with Trebbaino Toscano or other grapes, and these produce a very different wine.

**TASTING NOTES:** Trebbaino d'Abruzzo sparkles in my glass, transparent, brilliant, a light straw-yellow color with green tinges. It reminds me of summer sun reflected off a hillside meadow, captured in your glass, and of a quote attributed to Galileo Galilei, "Wine is sunlight, held together by water."

Swirl and sniff. You will detect fresh aromas of apricot, grapefruit, jasmine and orange blossoms, anise and light spices, and perhaps pear and melon.

It is crisp and clean on the palate, with plenty of acidity and a citrusy minerality. You will taste flavors of green apple, apricot, tangerine, anise, and almond, and light notes of lemon. The mouthfeel is creamy. It finishes long with harmonious acidity.

Best served chilled, at fifty to fifty-five degrees Fahrenheit.

**FOOD PARINGS:** Trebbaino d'Abruzzo is an excellent aperitif, transitioning to complement vegetable appetizers and crudites.

We love it with freshwater fish and seafood, especially steamed with herbs and finished with lemon butter, or with citrusy seafood pasta.

Its racy acidity means it pairs well with fried foods, as well. Try it with a vegetable tempura!

Trebbiano d'Abruzzo is at its best with the classic antipasti and pastas of the Roman trattoria, including baccalà, frutti di mare, bruschetta, spaghetti alla carbonara, bucatini all'amatriciana, and fettucini alfredo. We also like it with risottos with simple, minimal ingredients, such as risotto Milanese.

On a hot summer day, try Trebbaino d'Abruzzo with an orzo salad like Paolo creates. Combine cooked orzo with some peppers, olives, celery, and carrots, with an Italian-based dressing including one of my favorite cheeses, pecorino. Paolo finishes dinner with some shrimp, simply sautéed in garlic, butter, and sea salt, served over a small portion of jasmine rice.

For something very special, Paolo and I suggest this grilled lobster: Split or butterfly the lobster tails, shell and all, from head to tail. Drizzle the insides with a mixture of olive oil, lemon juice, salt, and pepper, and let it marinate for just a few minutes.

Grill the lobster tails on one side, cut side down, for five minutes; then add a bit more marinade and grill for another five minutes. The exact timing will depend, of course, on the size of your lobster; for doneness, check to see that the tail flesh is opaque and quite firm to the touch.

Now serve the lobster in its shell, with a bit more marinade drizzled on top. Melt-in-your-mouth perfection, especially when paired with this Trebbaino d'Abruzzo.

# Pecorino
## Back from the Brink of Extinction—Inspired by Estate Tiberio Pecorino

**STORY:** I have finally gotten to the Abruzzo seacoast, as Paolo promised. We've eschewed the hustle and bustle of Pescara for one of the many smaller towns that dot the coast, former fishing villages, grown larger with inns and resorts, catering to sun worshippers and those who want to relax by the sea. I've soaked in the sun, working on my tan, and swum in the clear blue-green sea. We've chased each other over the sand and into the water, and then retreated to our lounge chairs, to cool off in the fresh sea breezes.

Later that afternoon, as the day has moved into evening, we are sitting in a seaside café, our toes in the sand, turquoise waters lapping softly on the striking white beach in front of us. The scent of pine forests mixes deliciously with the scents of the sun and the sea. Sergio, Paolo's friend and former roommate at university, and his girlfriend, Francesca, who is also a cousin of Paolo's, join us. They are good friends, and we look forward to an afternoon and evening of good food, good wine, and good conversation.

Sergio is from Abruzzo and clearly loves his home. He tends to be very opinionated about wine and food, especially on his "home turf." I think he and Paolo have a friendly rivalry over food and wine knowledge and "what's best." So the question is, of the two, who will make the suggestions for our meal?

Meanwhile, Francesca and I are trading "girl talk." She has an innate sense of fashion, and I want to know where she found that incredible bikini, and the hat and dress she is now wearing. "Oh, this? Just a simple cover-up," she says. "Let's go shopping tomorrow; I'll show you something Paolo will love…on you."

Our waiter appears. "Let's start with a bottle of Pecorino," Sergio says. "The Estate Tiberio."

I'm suddenly confused. Pecorino, that's cheese, isn't it?

Sergio continues. "The antipasti plate to begin, and please, also include some pecorino on the plate."

Now I'm really confused.

"Sergio," I ask, "isn't pecarino the name of cheese made with sheep's milk?"

"Yes," he says, "that's true, but it's also the name of an old grape from this region of Italy. It makes a wonderful white wine, at once ancient and at the same time very new. It's a fascinating story. Would you like to hear it?"

Of course I say, "Yes."

"Local folklore says that shepherds used to guide their flocks down from the high mountain pastures, where they had spent their summers, to lower mountain pastures when these grapes were ripening and ready for picking. It seems the sheep not only relished these grapes as a treat, but the grapes also gave the sheep renewed energy. Another less evocative story is that shepherds and farmers planted and cultivated these grapes in the mountain pastures because they could thrive in the high elevations. As the shepherds moved their sheep between pastures, the sheep would browse on the grapes wherever they could. Science tells me this is probably due to the relatively high sugar content of the grapes. Because the sheep loved these grapes, they came to be known as 'pecorino,' from the Italian word for sheep, 'pecora.'"

I nod, as this makes sense to me. "But why haven't I ever heard of this wine?"

"Ah," says Sergio. "Simple economics. Despite the fact this is an ancient and hardy grape, is resistant to many diseases, would ripen at higher altitudes, and makes a very good wine, it is very low yielding. Therefore, in recent times, it has been replaced in vineyards by higher-yielding grapes like Trebbaino, as farmers sought to produce more volume and thus greater profit from their vineyards.

"By the mid-twentieth century, the Pecorino grape was thought to be extinct." Sergio shakes his head, sadly.

Our bottle of chilled Pecorino and antipasti and pecorino arrive. Sergio lifts a glass in a toast "But as you can taste, it was not lost to history after all!"

Our feast is ordered: roasted sardines with garlic and mint, steamed mussels, seafood pasta, and a dish that I can only describe as chicken thighs cooked to melt-in-your-mouth perfection with red pepper and onion. We have lots of crusty bread, still warm and fragrant from the oven, which I eat entirely too much of as I soak up the juice the mussels have steamed in. And of course, we enjoy another bottle of that Pecorino, which complements everything perfectly.

Over dinner, Sergio continues his story. "The savior and champion of Pecorino was a Marche farmer and vintner named Guido Cocci Grifoni. His daughter, Marilena, who stills runs the family vineyard, told me this story. Her father was something of a trailblazer in the region. He thought the white grapes being cultivated for wine, mainly Trebbaino Toscano, Malvasia, and Passerina, produced an inferior product that could not compete with the rest of Italy. So, in the early 1980s, he went looking for a 'new' grape by researching native white varieties. Rather than combing the fields and hillsides, he and his team dusted off old records. There he found mention of an old mountain grape known as Pecorella or Pecorino. And they discovered there still existed a tiny and virtually abandoned mountainside vineyard, located about thirty-three hundred feet above sea level, owned by an eighty-year-old man. Grifoni visited the vineyard in 1982 and came back to his farm with cuttings of this old Pecorino."

Sergio continues, "Grifoni grafted the cuttings onto modern rootstocks, planting the vines in various locations, to determine where they grew best. It took until the early 1990s before he had a harvest sufficient to make wine. However, after tasting the first vintage, he knew he had found the grape to make white wine as good as or better than any in Italy. He became determined to make Pecorino his star white. He continued to take cuttings and expand his plantings of Pecorino. Nearby vintners, however, did not share the same vision. His daughter told me that everybody thought Mr. Grifoni was a crazy man.

"Disappointed he could not convince neighbors to rip out their Trebbaino and Malvasia and plant Pecorino, he ventured into the neighboring region of Abruzzo, looking for a partner. Here he found a vintner who felt the same way about the problems with Trebbaino—sour and sometimes bitter, producing inferior wine. This kindred spirit recognized that Grifoni might have found a solution with the native Pecorino grape. So the two men took samples of the wine and vines to the local producers in Abruzzi, and they sold a million vines! The Abruzzi vintners believed in the new grape, even if those in Marche did not. This is why, today, people still think Pecorino comes from Abruzzi."

Sergio concludes, "So you see, we in Abruzzo are much smarter than our cousins in Marche to the north."

We all raise our glasses to thank Guido Grifoni for his part in rescuing this grape from extinction, and thus allowing us to enjoy one of the best white wines produced in Italy today.

I think of this story, and the Abruzzo seacoast, whenever I open a bottle of Pecorino.

**DESCRIPTION:** Pecorino is an ancient variety that has always called the mountains Apennine ridges of the Marche and Abruzzo its home. Thanks to the efforts of one man, Guido Cocci Grifoni, Pecorino was brought back from the brink of extinction in the 1980s. This low-yielding variety produces grapes that, when planted on the mountain hillsides it is native to, produce a wonderful high-quality white wine. In fact, a Pecorino took "Best Italian White" at the 2010 International Wine Challenge in London.

The wine is rich and glycerol heavy but also endowed with high total acidity, thereby offering a unique combination of texture and vibrancy. Due to the surging popularity of Pecorino wines, some vintners have planted the grape on the coast flatlands—but beware—the grape does best and produces the best wines from higher-elevation vineyards, like those of Estate Tiberio. If you can't find Estate Tiberio Pecorino, do check, if possible, on the location of the vineyard, choosing wine from vintners who use mountain-grown grapes. This will reward you with classic Pecorino.

Estate Tiberio harvests its Pecorino grapes at the end of September, crushes them and collects the free-run juice. This is fermented in stainless-steel tanks to preserve the unique Pecorino taste.

Pecorino is also that rare white that's worthy of the cellar. It can be aged successfully for more than ten years because of the structure of the wine. There's high acidity, plus the alcohol, that allows it to gain complexity over time. The acidity mellows but remains there.

I've found Pecorino to be a very versatile wine, good for simply sipping by itself or matching with food. Because it's complex and full-bodied, it can stand up to rich meals. In fact, Sergio describes it as "a red wine dressed in white."

**TASTING NOTES:** A classic Pecorino wine, like this one from Estate Tiberio, is dry and minerally, straw-yellow in color in your glass. It has an intense and elegantly floral bouquet of acacia and jasmine, with some citrus overtones, and sometimes spiced with a faint hint of licorice. Complex and full-bodied, the flavors are of sage, rosemary, green fig, peach, and yellow melon, with a long, lingering minerality.

**FOOD PAIRINGS:** This is a delightful aperitif wine, perfect on a warm day. Because of its complexity, it's more than just the average white "summer sipper"—enjoy and savor it with someone special, someone who will appreciate this special wine, its history, and the memories you are creating.

Of course, pecorino is a wonderful food wine as well, complementing a wide variety of dishes, from cheese to pasta and legumes, to white meat and seafood of all types.

We're very partial to serving "Pecorino and Pecorino"—with walnut bread when we can find or make it.

If you can find fresh sardines or similar small oily fish such as smelt, try roasting them with garlic and mint. The acidity and herbal flavors of the wine are perfect with this.

Try it paired with steamed white fish with ginger, or for a taste of Abruzzo, chicken thighs with roasted red pepper and onion, perhaps spiked with a couple pepperoncini or some red chili flakes.

Pecorino is absolutely sublime with pasta. One afternoon, Paolo and I cooked up some shrimp pasta with basil, garlic, and a homemade fresh tomato sauce, the tomatoes barely warm—and found it a perfect marriage for this Pecorino. The acidity in the wine complemented the tomato sauce very well, and the fruit and herbal aromatics mixed in wonderfully with the fresh shrimp and sprigs of basil.

Like steamed mussels? Try this Abruzzi-style version of *pepeta di cozza* (mussels in pepper broth). Rinse and scrub mussels under cold water. In a large pot, combine white wine, shallots, garlic, and salt. Simmer five minutes on medium heat. Add mussels, cover, and increase heat to high. Cook until all mussels are open, about five minutes. Stir in dried chili-pepper flakes and butter. Remove from heat. Discard any mussels that do not open. Garnish with parsley and serve with fresh, crusty bread.

## Region: Puglia

**Wines:**

- Sangiovese
- Primativo
- Negroamaro
- Salento Rosé

**Wineries:**

- Loggia dei Franchi
- Tenute Rubino
- Canaletto
- Cantele

# Puglia

## Land of Aeneas, Sun, and Sea

———— ❧ ————

SOMETIMES KNOWN AS Apulia, Puglia is the "Heel of Italy." It lies in the heart of the Mediterranean, flanked by the Adriatic Sea along its length and touching the Ionian Sea at its tip. Generally speaking, it is relatively flat, although there are areas of gently rolling hills such as those within the famous Valle D'Itrea. At its heart, however, it is a land of lush olive trees, vineyards, and wheat fields; of rich brown and red soils; of mild, wet winters and hot, dry summers; and of friendly, open people with ready smiles.

Puglia is a land of contradictions where pines grow side by side with palms. It is, at the same time, both a complex and a simple land, where tradition and history mix, oddly yet somehow comfortably, with technology and the modern world.

In many places, we discover that life goes on in Puglia as though the twenty-first century had never arrived. People live as their grandparents did: a bit of farming or fishing in the morning, a siesta from one o'clock to six o'clock (it's worth noting that nothing is open after lunch), and in the evening, a swim, perhaps, a gentle promenade through town, and then a slow, hearty meal made from local ingredients.

Thanks to Puglia's porous but mineral-rich limestone soil, proximity to the sea, and hot summers, this is where Italy's most delicious food is produced: big, fat, purple and green figs; long stems of velvet-red tomatoes; bunches of herbs still dusted with salt from the air; artichokes that thrive in sandy coastal fields; and peppers so sweet they are served as a sort of pudding at the end of a feast. Grand it is not, but bountiful it is.

Sometimes referred to as the "breadbasket" of Italy, Puglia historically produced much of Italy's pasta, and today it still produces over half of its olive oil. Increasingly, it is also becoming known for its rich, fruity red wines, particularly those from its Salento region at the bottom of the heel.

As you would expect, food plays an important part in Pugliese culture, and its main dishes are distinguished by an explosion of flavor in its meat and pasta dishes, often through the use of freshly picked herbs and vegetables, invariably obtained from individual private gardens. Almost everyone seems to have their own small vineyard as well as the inevitable olive trees. Almond and fig trees are also often found in private gardens or even growing wild at the roadside.

Strategically located and blessed with a rich, fertile soil, Puglia has been a coveted possession for many a civilization. It is believed to have been settled by the Greeks as early as the eighth century BC, and the Romans, Turks, Saracens, and Spanish, among others, have also held claim to parts of Puglia at one time or another through its history. An ancient Greek dialect is still spoken in a few remote areas.

The architecture of Puglia is at once simple yet stunning, a mixture of Greek and Baroque. From a distance, many of the smaller towns appear as beautiful "walled" villages, many sitting atop hills, with church spires and towers often rising high above the rooftops. Close up, it becomes apparent that the town "walls" consist of near-solid rows of tall, terraced houses that not only define the town perimeter, but were also designed to allow the town to be more easily defended against the coastal pirates and bandits of old. Some towns are made from a golden stone, others from gray-and-white limestone. In many of the towns, the buildings and houses are all painted white, to reflect the hot summer sun.

The light in Puglia has a very special quality, casting everything in a soothing, temperate glow, like a blessing. In the evenings, as the lights come on, they glow golden against the purple sky, like a Christmas village.

Puglia is also the home of the *Trulli*, simple yet beautiful dwellings with conical stone roofs made entirely of local limestone. Built by peasant farmers, with some dating back to the fifteenth century, they are today highly sought-after—despite the need to make heavy investments in their restoration—by both local residents and well-to-do outsiders. Originally a practical way for the poor farmer to build a home, today's *Trulli* have taken on a magical character, like tiny personal castles, with a fairy-tale quality about them. One expects an elf, or perhaps a hobbit, to greet you at the door.

Yes, things are different in Puglia.

# Primitivo
## Liquid History—Inspired by Loggia dei Franchi Primitivo

**STORY:** "History," he says, raising the glass of deep-purple wine and swirling it slowly, "this is liquid history."

Marco Franchi should know. His family has been raising grapes and olives and making wine and olive oil in Puglia, the sun-drenched "heel" of Italy, for hundreds of years. They still live in a *masseria*, a fortified farmhouse built of the local white limestone in the early 1700s, rising tall and square with towers. It looks almost like a miniature castle, rising above the fields, groves, and vineyards. Marco has two stunning photographs of his family home on his living-room wall. In one, the masseria shines brilliant white in the sunlight, in stark contrast to the green and gold fields and vineyards surrounding it. In the other photo, taken on a moonlit night, the masseria glows softly against the night sky and the silhouetted vines. It looks, not surprisingly, like the one pictured on the bottle of Loggia dei Franchi wine standing on the table.

Marco is in a nostalgic mood tonight. He's just returned to Florence from a long visit home and has invited Paolo and I and several other friends over for a "coming back from home" party. Paolo and I settle back for a virtual tour through some of the history and places of his homeland. We are planning a trip to Puglia, and this is a tantalizing introduction. Marco's "tour" takes us across the southern half of Puglia. He starts on the southern coast, at Porto Badisco, a beautiful rocky cove. He tells us that, according to legend, this is where Italy's mythological founder, Aeneas, landed. We end in Manduria, a city founded by the Greeks. Today, it is known as "The City of Primitivo." Just outside the present city is an ancient well, written about by Pliny the Elder in the first century AD. The well's water level is always constant, and an almond tree still grows out of its center, just as Pliny described almost two thousand years ago.

The tastes, however, are anything but virtual. The red wine is a Primitivo from Puglia, from the Franchi estate. A wealth of antipasti—spicy salami, olives, curls of sharp pecorino cheese, and little "no-meat meatballs" (fried balls of an eggplant mixture, served with a spicy chili pepper tomato sauce)—are arrayed on a platter. There is fragrant focaccia, with Franchi family olive oil for dipping. Marco surprises us with his favorite *bombette di maiale*—thin slices of pork wrapped around grated cheese, cured ham, or sausage, mixed with rosemary, skewered into a ball ("bomb"), and grilled. Orechiette pasta, served with our choice of either broccoli rabe sautéed with garlic in olive oil, or a spicy tomato-and-meat sauce, rounds out the feast.

Marco looks deep into his wine as he continues his story. "The Greeks settled in Puglia in the eighth century BC," he says, pausing thoughtfully as he looks up from his glass. "It is quite likely they brought this grape vine with them, for they certainly made wine in Puglia, as they did in Greece. Perhaps they brought it to the islands along the Croatian coast, or maybe it was the Romans, a little later. You can still find Roman ruins there, along the Croatian coast—amphitheaters and temples and houses."

He pauses again to take a sip and smiles. "It was Benedictine monks in the early 1600s who first recorded the name of this grape as 'Primitivo,' which means first or early one, because it is the first grape to ripen in September, full of the warmth of the sun, cooled by the breezes from the Aegean and Ionian Seas. It's still called that today in Italy." He looks at me and nods. "You know it in California, in America, as Zinfandel. In Croatia, on one small island, there are a handful of vines in a very old vineyard that are known as 'Crljenak Kaštelanski.' DNA testing recently showed them all to be genetically the same.

"Did you know," he asks, looking at me, "that Zinfandel, or 'Zenfendel,' was brought to America in 1820 as a cutting from the Imperial Austrian Plant Species Collection? Perhaps it was named after the Austrian who brought it from Italy or Croatia to Austria for the collection, or more likely, it was named after the person who imported it from Austria. No one knows for certain. It was first propagated in New York State and then quickly spread, going west to California with the Gold Rush."

I shake my head. "No, I didn't know that history."

"Take a sip," he says. We swirl, inhale, and slowly run the Primitivo over our tongues. "This is what a Zinfandel *would* taste like—*if* it were grown in the Puglia soil, under the hot Puglia sun, caressed by the Mediterranean sea breezes. *And if* it were made as we make it in Puglia, without any oak aging, to allow the true beautiful flavors of the grape to shine." He laughs. "Ah, but one can only find true Primitivo in Puglia!"

**DESCRIPTION:** This is a big red wine, made in the traditional style, rich, concentrated, and full-bodied. It is relatively high in alcohol, about 13–14 percent, with strong tannins, and intensely flavored. It is not aged in oak, so the true flavors of the grape prevail. In the glass, it is a dark, intense ruby red, almost inky. It is a luscious, mouth-filling wine, meant to be enjoyed with food.

Primitivo is the "flagship" grape of Puglia. Loggia dei Franchi creates this wine from grapes grown on old "alberello" vines in the Manduria region of Puglia. Alberello vines are shrub-like vines that grow without trellises, a growing style that has been used in Puglia for centuries. Interestingly, Zinfandel growers in Sonoma Valley have recently begun using the alberello style of growing, perhaps because this is how Primitivo is traditionally grown.

Loggia dei Franchi Primitivo is ready to enjoy now, as a relatively young wine, for its vibrant fruitiness. However, it will also continue to mature very nicely over the next five years, and it has good aging potential for even longer cellaring—if you can bear to store it away that long!

As with any good red wine, please open and allow the wine to breathe for about an hour to release the full flavors and aromas. I recommend serving at sixty-two to sixty-five degrees Fahrenheit.

**TASTING NOTES:** Primitivos tend to be juicy, well-structured, heavily colored, and rich wines, and this Loggia dei Franchi is no exception. As you swirl it in your glass, the aromas released will be of red berries and blackberries, with hints of spices and licorice. Close your eyes, and you may even smell the good red earth of Puglia, the sun and the sea, and warm breezes carrying the scents of ripe fruits. The taste will mirror the nose—deep-red cherries and berries, wild blackberries, and plums. There are hints of spices, perhaps cloves and anise, and the summer earth. It is smooth, velvety almost, with a delicious fruity finish.

**FOOD PAIRINGS:** This is a wine meant for "real food." It has been described as a masculine wine, and perhaps that is accurate. We know it's the perfect complement for big, bold, full-flavored, and spicy cuisine. If you're looking for a wine to pair with those barbequed beef ribs, this would be that wine!

It also goes well with the simple yet full-flavored and rustic cuisine from Puglia, of course. Try it with eggplant parmigiano, cold cuts and sharp or ripe cheeses, flavored focaccia, lentil or other bean soups, pasta with robust meat sauces, or roast lamb with onions and potatoes.

Or join Marco and friends and recreate that special dinner—savory fried eggplant balls, with a spicy tomato sauce as part of the antipasti, bombette di maiale, and orecchiette with cime di rapa (broccoli rabe or rapini cooked and sautéed with garlic) for something truly different—just like Puglia and this Primitivo wine!

# *Sangiovese*
## *Things Are Different in Puglia — Inspired by Loggia dei Franchi Sangiovese*

**STORY:** Things are different in Puglia. Paolo and I traveled to southern Italy, to Puglia, for the sun and the sea and for the food and the wine. And, to learn the story of a town where McDonald's couldn't stay in business.

Puglia stretches almost 250 miles, with over 500 miles of coastline on the Adriatic and Ionian Seas, offering golden sandy beaches, rocky coves, and turquoise waters. Inland from the coast, Puglia is classic, picture-postcard beautiful, with slightly rolling farmland—ancient, gnarled olive trees, vineyards, and wheat fields behind low stone walls.

Almost half of Italy's olive oil originates in Puglia, as does most of Italy's pasta, including the Puglian specialty, orecchiette ("little ears"). With some forty different grape varietals grown here, Puglia produces 15–20 percent of all Italian wine, some incredibly good, in fact award-winning, if not well-known. And the bread, ah, the bread—but we'll come to that in a minute!

Paolo and I are going to spend the day at Altamura. Altamura is a good-sized hill town in Puglia, about thirty miles inland, in the rocky interior known for sheep-farming. With a population of some seventy thousand and a good tourist industry, with a famous cathedral dating from the 1200s, it would seem like a good spot for a McDonald's to thrive. Indeed, one opened there in the central piazza in 2001, after careful analysis concluded that Altamura possessed the right size, diversity, and economy to support such a popular convenience. But Altamura's discriminating culinary tastes and liking for tradition presented some unexpected challenges to the newcomer.

For one thing, Altamura is famous for its bread, which is sold in numerous other Italian cities. Altamura bread was the first baking product in Europe to be granted a DOP certificate and is so far the only Italian bread to qualify for the honor. (DOP stands for Denominazione d'Origine Protetta, or denomination of protected origin, the equivalent of DOC

[Denominazione di Origine Controllata, or denomination of controlled origin], used for wines.) The bread is made from locally grown durum wheat flour with yeast, water, and marine salt, according to a recipe dating to 1500, although the formula is almost certainly older. Horace, the Roman poet living in the first century BC, called the bread of Altamura "the best in the world." It is baked in an open wood-fired oven. Anyone care for a microwaved egg McMuffin instead?

Across the central piazza in Altamura from where the ill-fated franchised McDonald's restaurant once stood is Luigi Di Gesu's bakery. His family has baked bread here in Altamura for hundreds of years. We sat outside the bakery with Signor Di Gesu himself, sharing a thick slice of his signature focaccia, one of his famous panini, and a bottle of good Sangiovese wine from Puglia. The label on the bottle was quintessential Puglia—a sketch of rolling vineyards and a masseria, which is a large, fortified farmhouse. These are hundreds of years old and built of white limestone. We are staying in one, just outside Altamura.

I take a sip and look at Paolo, who is smiling and nodding. I know immediately we'll be drinking more of this wine again, probably at dinner, with pasta, and perhaps some grilled lamb.

"I had not set out to force McDonald's to close," Luigi says. "It was simply a question of free choice."

After only two years, it seems, in 2002, McDonald's retreated from Altamura, taking down the Golden Arches citing "lack of profitability." It was hailed by some as a victory for local European cuisine over globalized fast food.

Luigi chuckles and adds, "I merely offered the residents and visitors my tasty focaccia and filled panini, which they seem to have overwhelmingly preferred to industrial hamburgers and chicken nuggets."

As we sipped the simple, rustically elegant, unoaked Sangiovese, full of the goodness of the Puglian sun and earth, and enjoyed the rustic focaccia and the panini filled with one of Signor Di Gesu's specialty blends of scamorza cheese, eggs, basil, and tomato, we could understand why, and wholeheartedly agreed.

Still today, a glass of a good Sangiovese from Puglia, like that Loggia dei Franchi Sangiovese, takes me back to Altamura and Signor Di Gesu and the delicious and comforting country cuisine of Puglia. And I remember my adventures in Puglia with Paolo, traveling the beautiful country roads that meander from sunlit beaches through silvery olive groves and green vineyards to charming inland towns, and to that masseria we stayed in outside of Altamura.

**DESCRIPTION:** Loggia dei Franchi Sangiovese is a great example of the most famous Italian grape varietal. Sangiovese is perhaps better known as the primary grape used in Chianti and many Super Tuscans, but grown here in sunny Puglia, it makes a very different style of wine. This wine captures the heart of the dignified, smooth northern Sangiovese grape, but with a good measure of southern soul added in. The climate in Puglia is always warm and sunny, so the wines that come from there are quite different in characteristics from the wines made farther north in places such as Tuscany or Piedmonte. They are more "sun-kissed" in style and show this by exhibiting an abundance of juicy fruit flavors. And so, this Sangiovese from Puglia is a gentle red wine, medium-bodied, easy to drink and enjoy with many foods, and yet, it comes at a very affordable price.

Loggia dei Franchi Sangiovese wine is specially selected from top vineyard plots of mature, low-yielding vines, grown in the "alberello" style in the Salento peninsula. Alberello are shrub-like vines, grown without trellising, a growing style that has been used in Puglia for centuries. The wine is left deliberately unoaked to make a juicy, easy-drinking red wine, full of the character and luscious flavors of the Sangiovese grape. This Sangiovese is meant to be drunk young, no aging needed. Open, let breathe, and enjoy with food and friends, served at a temperature of sixty to sixty-five degrees Fahrenheit.

**TASTING NOTES:** Loggia dei Franchi Sangiovese is a wonderful everyday wine—unpretentious yet with a simple elegance, and a great food-friendly wine. As you pour it into your glass, you'll notice its intense, deep ruby-red to purple color. Aromas of red berries and cherries, overlaid the perfume of warm violets, will delight your nose. Take a sip—a perfect blend of cherries and plums, fresh and lively, with a hint of spiciness—the essence of the Sangiovese grape, grown sensuous and luscious in the sun of Puglia. The tannins are soft and ripe, and the acidity clear and balanced. Overall, a wonderful harmony on the palate.

**FOOD PAIRINGS:** This Loggia dei Franchi Sagiovese just might be the perfect partner for pizza and pasta, as well as most other Mediterranean-style dishes. It will elevate a pizza margharita from "simple" to "simply delicious." If you enjoy spicy pizzas, full of sausage, pepperoni, and other savory treats, this Sangiovese is the perfect accompaniment.

We think you'll find a Puglia Sangiovese pairs exceptionally well with meat antipasti, as well as bruschetta, with pasta with spicy tomato-based sauces, such as penne alla puttanesca, and with hearty vegetarian fare like baked eggplant with mozzarella and tomato.

Try it with almost any roasted or grilled meat, including wild game. It transports us back to those little whitewashed towns in Puglia, such as Cisternino, where, at night, numerous butchers set up tiny tables on the sidewalks and cook to order, over coals or in wood-fired ovens, whatever you select from their marble counters, preceded by minuscule black olives, homemade cheeses, and salami.

If you're feeling adventurous, you might like to try your hand at one of Puglia's pasta specialties—*maccheroni al forno*. The maccheroni is mixed with meatballs, hard-boiled eggs, and all manner of other ingredients—usually some vegetables, cheeses, and whatever else strikes the cook's fancy. Finally it is topped with a pie crust and baked in the oven to produce a sensationally rich and tasty dish.

# Negroamaro
## Flamingoes and the Tarantella — Inspired by Cantele Negroamaro

**STORY:** Whenever I drink a Puglian wine, especially a Negroamaro, I remember how I learned the tarantella. It all started with the flamingoes.

There we were, at the salt pans in the Natural Reserve at Torre Colimena, marveling at the sight of over five hundred flamingos, brilliantly pink against the turquoise and lapis blue of the water and sky. I never knew there were flamingos in Europe, having only associated them with Florida and Africa. Paolo strikes up a conversation with another young couple, Francesco and Sophia, who are also gawking at the huge, ungainly looking, yet improbably elegant birds. We seem to hit it off immediately and soon find ourselves lunching with them at a small and intimate trattoria.

The four of us select a variety of dishes from the menu—*pizzette* (miniature pizza), zuccini Scapese (zucchini fingers lightly breaded, fried, and splashed with red wine or balsamic vinegar), pickled baby tomatoes and peppers, artichokes marinated in lemony oil, zucchini-blossom fritters filled with sheep's-milk ricotta, polpette (deep-fried balls of octopus, cheese, bread crumbs, and eggs) served on wafer-thin vegetables drizzled with olive oil, and Caprese salad. These delectable treats are eagerly shared between us.

Our new friends select the wine, a Cantele Negroamaro. "We have a saying in Puglia," Francesco says, "the better the wine, the less it costs." He goes on to explain that this is because Puglia reds, such as this Negroamaro, are traditionally meant to be enjoyed rather young. Today they are fermented and aged in stainless-steel vats, which is of course less costly than aging in small oak barriques. It also allows the character of the grape to come through. The Negroamaro is a perfect match for our meal.

One thing leads to another as we converse over our extended lunch. We invite them to visit us in Florence; Francesco and Sophia invite us to their wedding, which is just a few days away and will take place in Locorotondo, a hilltop village town about ten miles inland from the

Adriatic coast, situated at the top of the Salento peninsula. Often referred to as "the balcony on the Valle d'Itria" because of its position 1350 feet above sea level, Locorotondo offers beautiful views of the countryside, which is dotted with the cone-shaped trulli unique to that area of Puglia. The timing is perfect, and we graciously accept.

Locorotondo, founded in AD 1000, is a *borgo più bella d'Italia*—that is, it's rated as one of the most beautiful towns in Italy. It's easy to see why. Locorotondo is known for its round historical center, from which derives its name, meaning "round place". The town is built on a circular plan with narrow concentric streets and alleys, paved with ivory stone, forming a labyrinth. The terraced houses are whitewashed, with unusually steep pitched roofs, tiled with limestone slabs. The effect is almost otherworldly. Everything is shimmering white, punctuated by bloodred geraniums and petunias that tumble from window boxes and spill over wrought-iron balconies. Here, art is not a masterpiece hung in a museum, but an entire town.

It is a magical place for the wedding, which is held in the Chiesa Madre di San Giorgio (The Mother Church of Saint George), which occupies the center of the old town. We learned the church was built between 1790 and 1825. On the facade, there is a relief of "St. George and the Dragon" above the entrance, and inside, one of the most beautiful cupola domes I've ever seen.

After the ceremony, we join the wedding celebration, which spills into the piazza. Of course, no Italian wedding or celebration would be complete without the rhythmic song and dance of the tarantella. Remember the wedding in the movie *The Godfather*? If so, you may recall the tarantella. The tarantella may be the most popular of all the Italian songs, both lively and graceful. The accompanying dance is one of light and quick steps mixed with passionate gestures.

To fully appreciate the experience Paolo and I so thoroughly enjoyed that day, I will have to share with you some of the history we learned about the tarantella. It was told to us by one of Sophia's sisters, who seemed to find Paolo most attractive. She poured all of us another glass of wine and explained, "There are two types of tarantella dances, dating back to the Middle Ages.

"The more stately courtship tarantella is danced by a couple or couples, and is graceful and elegant." Valentina smiles at Paolo. "This dance originated in Puglia and spread through southern Italy. It's said that in the fifteenth century, the original dance was changed by a fusion with the Spanish fandango, and also the Moresca—a couples or group dance in which the dancers mimed a sword combat between Christians and Muslims.

"And then there is the 'curative' tarantella. It was danced solo by a supposed victim of a spider bite. However, the spider is not what you think of as a tarantula today. Rather, it was the *Lycosa tarantula,* a local variety of wolf spider. These spiders are large, ground-dwelling, agile hunters with excellent eyesight and are named after the town of Taranto in Puglia.

"This dance was agitated and even frenzied in character, and it lasted for hours or even several days. Musicians would play fast, lively music, and often townspeople would gather round to encourage and watch the dancer. This dance was done in order to sweat the venom out of the victim's pores, even though the spider's venom is not fatal to humans. It's sort of musical exorcism. My science teacher thinks it was probably the highly venomous Mediterranean black widow that was actually the spider responsible for the bites that caused the convulsions and delirium that occurred during the grain harvest, not the wolf spider."

In addition to the history lesson, Valentina takes it upon herself to teach us the tarantella. Fortified by several glasses of Negroamaro wine, we are soon bouncing and jumping and kicking with alternating feet. When the dance is in groups, the dancers form a circle and move clockwise while keeping the right hand toward the center and the left hand on the hip. In the couple's dance, we dance in front of each other, mirroring each other's movements, turning around each other while being shoulder to shoulder, or turning with arms locked while facing each other. Another variation has one partner kneeling, while the other dances sensuously around him or her. Valentina demonstrates, gyrating seductively, but I am a quick study, and with Paolo's encouragement, I soon resume my place as Paolo's dance partner.

The afternoon fades into the evening, with a lovely full moon rising over the town. We have eaten good food, sipped wonderful wine, and danced the tarantella and other more modern dances. We are relaxed but feeling very alive, and given the surroundings, rather romantically inclined. Paolo says, "Yes, perhaps they have it right in Puglia, where we can step into a town that time forgot, like in your musical *Brigadoon*. I think maybe we spend too much time staring into screens and not enough time drinking wine, tongue kissing, and dancing under the moon." We seem to have remedied any such shortcomings, at least for tonight.

**DESCRIPTION:** Like many Italian grapes, the origins of the Negroamaro plant itself are shrouded in the mists of history. It most likely was brought to Italy by Greek colonists in about the eighth century BC, where it found an ideal habitat in this hot, rocky, and arid region. What is certain about Negroamaro—one of Italy's most ancient vines—is that it has an ancestral bond with Puglia, and as the symbol of the Salento, is more than just a native vine.

Bearing this history in mind, the meaning of the name Negroamaro is probably from Greek and Latin roots, not Italian. The Italian translation would be "black" and "bitter." The more probable explanation is that the name Negroamaro derives from the fusion of the Greek word *maru* or *mavra* and the Latin word *nigrum*, both meaning "black" and referring to the colour of the grapes, so that Negroamaro actually means blackest of the black.

After being destemmed and crushed, the must macerates with skin contact for six to seven days. After fermentation, the wine is then aged in stainless-steel vats to preserve its fruity, fresh qualities.

Cantele Negroamaro wine is ready to drink, with delicate aromatic evolution over the next two to three years. As the wine ages, its flavors will evolve as its tannin mellows.

It's best served at sixty-one degrees Fahrenheit.

**TASTING NOTES:** Like tasting the southern Italian sunshine in a glass, this is a gorgeous, richly textured red wine with an abundance of ripe, sunsoaked fruit: cherry, blackcurrant, blueberry, and blackberry, along with hints of spices such as nutmeg and allspice and cinnamon, and dark cocoa. Other flavor notes you might detect include smoke, plum, and herbs, such as thyme, which may have been growing nearby, followed by a flinty minerality.

Cantele Negroamaro is medium-bodied, and the mouthfeel is striking: it feels, at times, like you're drinking silk. The tannins are medium yet soft. This wine is intensely friendly and approachable, starting out softly and evolving into a delicate yet confident finish.

It swirls intensely ruby red with tender, soft hints of violet in your glass.

**FOOD PAIRINGS:** Even though this Negroamaro is full-bodied, it is not too tannic or acidic, and instead leads with fruit, which makes it easy to love, especially alongside meatballs or pizza. True to its origins, it is perfect with most Mediterranean cuisine, pasta with sauce, especially spicy ones, soups, and gentle aged cheeses, and even the luxuriously creamy burrata.

If your antipasti tend toward the spicy, such as Calabrese salami, pepperoncini, or a spicy bruschetta with onions, garlic, and red peppers (pepperonata), this Cantele Negroamaro will complement it nicely.

We love it with foie gras served with fresh, ripe figs. A most decadent and luxurious appetizer.

Try this with tagliatelle al ragù for a match made in heaven, especially a lamb or goat ragù. Or Puglia style "orechietti," little pasta ears, with rapini and garlic, or cavatieddi alla ruca with rocket, tomato, and pecorino cheese.

The Negroamaro is also perfect with lamb—grilled lamb chops; kebabs; lamb chops baked wrapped in foil with onions, garlic, and olives; or slow-baked lamb and potatoes, a traditional meal in Puglia. It's simple, yet full of flavor and comfort. To make it, mix bread crumbs, parmesan, herbs of your choice (I'm partial to thyme and rosemary), and pepper. Pour a little olive oil in the bottom of a dutch oven. Layer waxy potatoes such as Yukon Gold in the bottom of the dutch oven; then add a layer of cubed lamb and a light layer of the bread-crumb mixture. Depending on how many you are feeding, you can repeat the layers, ending with bread crumbs. Add some white wine and another drizzle of olive oil, cover, and cook in a slow oven (300 to 325 °F) for an hour and a half to two hours, the last thirty minutes without the lid. This just perfumes the kitchen while cooking and will have you salivating.

On a summer evening, try this with grilled tuna steaks, cooked to a medium-rare perfection like a good steak. Simply baste tuna steaks with a mixture of thyme leaves, olive oil, sea salt, and lemon juice, and let them marinate for a couple of hours in the refrigerator. Grill them over hot coals along with some peppers and eggplants.

Spaghetti puttanesca—or "whore's spaghetti" as it's otherwise known—is a punchy pasta dish with strong, salty flavors. There are various theories as to how the dish got its name, the most plausible being that it was a simple dish that could be easily and quickly put together out of what was in the cupboard between clients' visits. The other popular theory is that the sauce was as spicy as one of the local "ladies of the evening." The sauce is made with a heady mixture of garlic, anchovies, capers, chilies, and olives with tomatoes. This can be quite a lot for a wine to handle, but a southern Italian red, like this Negroamaro, does it quite nicely.

And for something surprisingly good, try Cantele Negroamaro with spicy Indian cuisine such as chicken tikka masala.

# Rosé Salento
# When Only the Best Beaches Will Do —
# Inspired by Cantele Rosé Salentino

**STORY:** It might be winter, but with a bottle of Cantele Rosé Salentino, a few photos, and some well-prepared Puglian-style fresh seafood and pasta, Paolo and I are back in Puglia, on a white sand beach, feeling warm and sensuous from the sun and breeze and sea.

With more than five hundred miles of coast on two seas, the Adriatic and the Ionian, Puglia has all sorts of gorgeous beaches. The sea is a thousand shades of turquoise. The beaches range from a deep, warm gold to blinding white stretches of sand. Some front old and vibrant cities and towns, with rows of bright lounge chairs and umbrellas, and great night life. Some are in national parks and wildlife refuges, contrastingly quiet and natural, perfumed by pine trees and lavender. Other areas on the coast are rocky, with towering cliffs and stunning offshore rock formations reaching like white statues into the blue sky.

Paolo and I are "on a mission" to visit a few of the "best, most beautiful" beaches and to sample some of the bounty of the sea and land in Puglia. It's September, so the summer crowds of beach vacationers, and most tourists, are gone. We'll have some of those beaches all to ourselves.

We start in the north, at the beautiful Baia delle Zagare beach, between the small towns of Vieste and Mattinata. It is named after the flowers of the many citrus trees that are indigenous to the area. They scent the air with a wonderfully romantic orange and lemon-blossom perfume, a soft, sweet contrast to the slightly salty air, yin and yang, feminine and masculine. We hike down to the beach, a curving half mile or so of soft white sand, surrounded by a national park and a tall white limestone cliff. There are two distinctive white rock formations near the shore, one a stunning arch.

To our surprise and delight, there is no one there today but us.

We continue our way south. We have to stop in Polignano a Mare, Puglia's ice-cream mecca. Yes, it's before lunch, but we are heeding the sage advice of an old friend of mine, who often says, "Life is short; eat dessert first." And so, we are doing just that.

The beauty of the town, bisected by a dramatic ravine that leads to the sea, threatens to distract us from our goal—*Il Super Mago del Gelo* ice-cream shop, justly venerated for its fruit gelati and dark, slushy coffee granita. We sample three—a rich and decadent fig, an impossibly refreshing lemon, and the astounding *caffè-nocciola* gelato.

We move down the coast to Monopoli, its little harbor bay full of colorful fishing boats, yachts, and coastal sailing vessels. The city rises from steep, rocky cliffs and hides behind a seafront wall. It's a dense labyrinth of houses, markets, shops, churches, monasteries, and crypts spread around the port's idyllic harbor. A beautiful baroque cathedral completes the scene, guarded by the stunning seafront castle of Charles V.

A walk down the beach eventually brings us to a restaurant, Lido Bianco, perched on a hill dense with lavender and sea grass, overlooking the turquoise sea. We venture inside for a light lunch and are more than satisfied with our tuna and snapper tartare, sea urchin roe served in the urchin shell, fresh-caught grilled lobster, and salad, paired with a lovely rosé wine from the southern end of Puglia, Cantele Rosé Salento.

The afternoon finds us in the Torre Guaceto Marine Reserve, just north of Brindisi. I remember this beach not only for its baby-powder white sand, the schools of silvery fish flitting from reef-like rock formations in pools of crystal-clear water, and the scent of pine needles drifting from the pristine forest that borders the beach, but also for entertaining and memorable antics of some of the other visitors we meet there.

For example, as we approach a sheltered rocky basin where the beach curves and drops sharply into the sea, our attention is drawn by the loud scolding a father is giving his child. "I said put it back; this is a natural park," the stern father tells his son. He is pointing to the small octopus that sits with protruding eyes on the boy's shoulder after being plucked from the crystalline waters. "Oh, please, can't I keep him as a pet? He likes me!" pleads the boy. The father shakes his head. "No, no."

The octopus is soon returned to a rocky pool. Paolo and I smile and quietly walk away.

Heading south, we pass San Foce, an old fisherman's village. Yes, it has beautiful coves of clean white sand surrounded by white rock outcroppings, pristine water full of fish, and a series of little islets that can be easily reached swimming. We have come, however, to rent a boat, to visit one of the several grottoes or caves dotting the rocky shore, the beautiful Grotta degli Amanti (Cave of Lovers). Here, according to local legend, two young lovers took refuge when they were caught in a storm. Sadly, the winds and seas grew so violent that they died and were found when the storm cleared, still locked in a lover's embrace. The seas and winds are calm today, so we feel safe anchoring the boat just outside the entrance and plunging into the warm water to explore the cave.

Farther south, we come to Otranto, one of Puglia's most charming towns. It is also Italy's easternmost city, with a protected harbor. On a clear day, you can see Albania and Corfu. Because of this, it has been a point for invasions from across the Adriatic. This story is best illustrated in the city's Romanesque cathedral, built in 1088. On display in a glass case behind the altar are the bones of 813 Christian martyrs, massacred by the Ottoman Turks in 1480 when, after the city fell to a siege, they took refuge in the Cathedra, and refused to convert to Islam. Less macabre is the cathedral's other showstopper, extensive twelfth-century floor mosaics that rival the famous early Christian mosaics of Ravenna in richness and historical significance.

There is also an imposing castle, with thick perimeter walls and robust towers, built after the town was liberated from the Turks in the late fifteenth century, which dominates much of the town and its small port, as well as the seafront promenades replete with excellent fish restaurants alongside the town's very own beautiful white sandy beach and sky-blue waters.

We, however, pass up the Otranto beaches, lovely as they are, for the fingerlike cove of Porto Badisco, a few miles south. According to myth, this is a magical beach. Virgil, the ancient Roman poet, told the story of how Aeneas, the son of the goddess Venus, and a hero of the Trojan War, fled after the fall of Troy. He and some other surviving followers landed here. Their descendants became the founders of Rome.

The pebble beach provides beautiful views and shady spots perfect for picnics. We've packed a basket with pecorino cheese, some salami, sardines, and *taralli*, Italy's answer to the pretzel. Small and circular, these crackers make for a wonderful snack. We have selected several savory flavors—fennel, black peppercorn, and poppy seed. And, of course, wine—another bottle of Cantele Rosé Salentino, which we've managed to keep nicely chilled in our little cooler. Our basket includes two wine glasses and a cork screw. We toast Venus.

The southern tip of the Salento peninsula is dramatic—white limestone cliffs spotted with the deep green of gnarled pine trees, Paleolithic grottoes, and coves of powder-white sand and azure sea. At the very bottom of Italy's stiletto, where the Adriatic and Ionian Seas meet, is the cape of Santa Maria di Leuca. Nearby, at the Fiordo del Ciolo, bold divers leap from a bridge into the brilliant blue waters of the narrow bay, aptly titled "fjord," some ninety feet below. There is only a tiny beach at the end of the little fjord. I manage to persuade Paolo to continue on rather than try cliff diving.

Gallipoli, our next stop, is a two-part town: the modern hub is based on the mainland, while the older *centro storico* inhabits a small island that juts out into the Ionian Sea. With serene baroque architecture, it is, arguably, the prettiest of Salento's smaller settlements. We spend our time in the old town, ringed by the remains of its muscular fourteenth-century walls. There are several baroque chapels, a traditional fishing port, a windswept sea drive, and narrow lanes barely wide enough to accommodate our tiny Fiat.

Happy hour, *aperitivo,* finds us at one of the many seaside bars, Riviera Armando Diaz. We have drinks and snacks—bruschetta, frittata, fried seafood, and stuffed pasta. The DJ matches his musical selection with the incredible atmosphere—a sunset over the water that is to die for, combined with the swank decor of the outdoor terrace lounge. It makes us feel as though we are "living the dream," and perhaps we are.

Much later, we have dinner at Il Bastione. The owner and chef, Marcello Caricola, is so obsessed with fresh seafood that he walks twice a day to the harbor where fishermen sell their catch, "Because," he explains, "some fish, like lobster and urchins, are best caught in the morning, others, like the pesce azzurro, in the evening."

Perhaps that is why Marcello's seafood is, without doubt, the best we have tasted in all of Puglia: a platter with chili and saffron prawns; tiny squid with an iridescent arugula puree; a swordfish wrap, stuffed with raisins, pinenuts, mint, and parmesan; delicately battered cod; grilled octopus served on a potato; and a specialty of Gallipoli, *gambieri crudi*—raw prawns served whole, similar to ceviche, doused in lemon juice with a slew of wonderful herbs and a touch of fragrant olive oil. There are two salads, one with celery and lemon zest, and a second with ribbons of zucchini and carrot topped with sundried tomatoes, mint, almonds, and pecorino cheese. We enjoy a bottle of Cantele Rosé Salentino, made from the Negroamaro grape.

We somehow find room to share a fresh fig tart for dessert.

We head north the next morning. The name says it all, *Porto Selvaggio*—"Wild Harbour." You can only get to Porto Selvaggio on foot, and this is probably what's kept it special. From the main entrance of the Port Selvaggio Natural Park preserve, it's about a twenty-minute walk downhill to the beach. Porto Selvaggio's intimate rocky beach is surrounded by pine forest. The sea here is incredible. It's crystal clear and packed with fish—there are shoals of them, as well as octopi and starfish. We imagine that in the summer, this would be an ideal place to escape the relentless Puglian sun—swim, then repair to the refreshing shade of the pine forest for a picnic, with a view of an imposing sixteenth-century defensive watchtower, the Torre Dell'Alto, just across the little bay

Our last stops are two beaches near the town of Maruggio, San Pietro in Bevagna and Le Dune di Campomarino. Both of these offer seclusion amid white sand dunes and lush beach vegetation—fragrant juniper, lavender, and thyme.

We stop first at the beach at San Pietro in Bevagna. Paolo reminds me that San Pietro in Bevagna is named for St. Peter, who, according to legend, was shipwrecked off the coast in a bad storm. He came ashore and made his way to the well in a small village, marked by a statue of the pagan god, Zeus.

On seeing the sculpture, St. Peter made the sign of the cross, and with that gesture, the statue shattered and fell in a thousand pieces at his feet. The people who witnessed this miracle converted to Christianity on the spot! The village grew, as people came from afar to visit the holy site of the miracle. An ancient church marking the site still stands in the town center.

Our last beach is Dune di Campo, where it is just the two of us and a bottle of Rosé Salentino. In such moments are the best memories made.

**DESCRIPTION:** Cantele Rosé Salentino is 100 percent Negroamaro. The grapes are harvested during the second half of December, and after crushing, they are macerated for twelve to twenty-four hours in order to extract the correct color from the skins and the classic aromatic notes of Negroamaro. The free-run must is fermented in stainless-steel vats, where it remains until alcoholic fermentation is completed. The wine is then aged in stainless steel until bottling. This produces a rosé of great character, a bouquet of fresh strawberries and ripe summer fruit.

Meant to be enjoyed upon release, it can be stored for one to two years. It's best served at fifty to fifty-two degrees Fahrenheit.

**TASTING NOTES:** Cantele Rosé Salentino is a soft, sensuous pink in color. On the nose, it is sweet and nuanced. Fragrant and fresh notes of violet, black cherry, and cherry alternate and meet with inviting and measured scents of pomegranate, raspberry, and strawberry, with hints of geranium and rose.

The wine's impressive alcohol is balanced by its delicate flavors and light, bright freshness, elegance, and persistence. It is at once fruity, marine, and mineral, and thanks to its roundness, it is remarkably pleasant to drink.

**FOOD PAIRING:** Cantele Rosé Salentino is perfect to sip on its own. It just might transport you to a secluded beach in Puglia, the sun warm on your face, the soft breeze, fragrant with pine and lavender, caressing your skin, the water inviting you in.

It will complement almost any seafood, any preparation—raw in the Puglian style, or ceviche or sushi; grilled on the barbeque, plain or spicy; fried;

baked in a salt crust; seafood risotto, seafood soup, seafood over pasta. It's also perfect with spicy BBQ chicken.

Vegetarian? This is excellent with cheese soufflé, quiche, vegetable torts, and eggs, poached or scrambled. We love this with eggs Benedict, especially a version made with crab or shrimp instead of Canadian bacon. For something different for dinner, try poached eggs over nicely cooked spaghetti-squash strands, bathed in a garlicky olive oil, with a toss of sun-dried tomato and a little goat cheese.

We also love this with Caprese salad, with juicy fresh tomatoes, soft fresh mozzarella, basil from the herb garden, and a splash of oil and balsamic vinegar. Or, if you can find it, *burrata*, a fresh, soft cheese that has to be eaten within twenty-four hours of production—absolutely delicious! It's soft, fresh mozzarella filled with stracciatella (soft mozzarella curds mixed with cream), additional cream, and sometimes soft butter. Unsurprisingly, it complements many of the sheep's milk cheeses Puglia is known for, such as pecorinos and ricottas.

# *Region: Sicily*

**Wines:**

    Nero d'Avola

    Fiano

    Aglianico

**Wineries:**

    Antica Cantina Pandiani

# Sicily

## The Sunlight of Sicily and the Fires of Mt. Etna

───── ⬙ ─────

AH, SICILY, THE largest of the Italian islands, off the "toe" of the Italian boot, surrounded by the Ionian, the Tyrrhenian, and the Mediterranean Seas. If the first thing that comes to mind when you hear the word "Sicily" is *The Godfather* and "Mafioso," please, let me expand your horizons. There is so much here to discover, much more than Mafiosi. For starters, there is Mt. Etna, the mountain of fire and ice—literally. The tallest active volcano in Europe, constantly smoking and spitting lava, Mt. Etna hosts two ski resorts on its north face.

Sicily is a land with a long history of human habitation, dating from as early as 12,000 BC. The Phoenicians settled here first, followed by Greeks, Carthaginians, and then the Romans. After the fall of the Roman Empire in the fifth century AD, this region was ruled by the Vandals, the Ostrogoths, the Byzantine Empire, and the Emirate of Sicily. Then came the Normans, leading to the creation of the Kingdom of Sicily, which was subsequently ruled by the Hohenstaufen, then the Spanish Capetian House of Anjou, the Hapsburgs, and lastly the House of Bourbon (French) with the Kingdom of Naples and the Kingdom of the Two Sicilies. Sicily finally became part of unified Italy in 1860.

Sicily might be one of the world's most captivating places. Among the island's innumerable charms are the ever-present scent of lemon trees, the purity of dawn light on terra-cotta walls, the colorful markets, the drama of Etna erupting against a darkening sky, the beautiful turquoise sea, the sense that history lurks always just around the next corner, the reflective marble glow of late-night streets, the exotic flavors of Sicilian food, reflecting its multicultural heritage, and of course, its wine.

# *Nero d'Avola*
## *The View from Taormina—Inspired by Antica Cantina Pandiani Nero d'Avola*

**STORY:** Paolo had surprised me with a long weekend trip to Sicily, his grand-mother's homeland. We stayed in Taormina, a charming hillside town on Sicily's east coast. Ever since Taormina fell to the Romans in 212 BC, it's been a favorite holiday and tourist destination. It boasts a beautiful harbor and views of Mt. Etna, a superb Greco-Roman amphitheater, a bounty of good restaurants, and vibrant nightlife.

Taormina has also been a source of inspiration to a long list of writers over the centuries, starting with Ovid and continuing to the present day. So, while Paolo spent some time skiing on Mt. Etna, I sought "inspiration" for writing.

I knew Goethe, the great German writer, poet, philosopher, and diplomat, traveled to Italy and Sicily in the 1780s. He wrote of these travels in his book *Italianische Reise (Italian Journey).* He praised Taormina to such a degree that it became an integral part of the *Grand Tour,* upon which fashionable English gentlemen and intellectuals embarked for purposes of education and refine-ment in the 1800s. Goethe said that the best view in all of Italy, or perhaps in all the world, was from the top of Taormina's Greco-Roman Theater. And the most famous, or infamous, visitor was perhaps D. H. Lawrence, who found at Taormina the inspiration for his feverishly sensual *Lady Chatterley's Lover.* He and his wife Frieda rented a villa here for about two years. According to local rumor, the story was based on Frieda's intimate dalliances with a Sicilian mule driver.

I discovered an interesting thing while wandering the streets of Taormina. The Corso Umberto is the main pedestrian street through Taormina and is hard to miss, lined with numerous high-end shops as well as gelato shops, produce vendors, cafés, souvenir shops, and jewelry shops. At night the street comes alive with music and entertainment, a blocks-long party. I found Taormina's little tourist shops do a brisk business in overpriced Sicilian crafts, to be expected, but also in postcard photos of sepia-toned nubile young men and women. These soft-core pictures, quite artistically done, are the work of the German artist and photographer, Baron Wilhelm von Gloeden, and date from the 1880s and 1890s. I can see how these photos tapped into the sensual fantasies of socially frustrated denizens from northern Europe longing for relief from the dreary winter months and an outlet for artistic or sexual energies. They still evoke that sense even today. Taormina becomes not so much a different place, but more a different state of mind. Sensuality pervades the warm sun, the lemon- and orange-blossom-scented air, the soft sea breezes, the incredible beauty. Worries dissolve; inhibitions loosen.

Lunch is a wonderful spread of eggplant caponata, carpaccio, and porcini risotto with sautéed foie gras, paired with a glass or two of a Sicilian Nero d'Avola wine from Antica Cantina Pandiani. Afterward, I treat myself to another Sicilian specialty, granita, a semifrozen icy dessert, at the justly famous BamBar. My only dilemma is choosing a flavor. I finally decide on peach. A little more sightseeing and shopping in town, and then, taking Goethe's advice, I make the long climb up to the Greek Amphitheater in the late afternoon.

The view is every bit as beautiful as Goethe described. I have my writer's notebook, but instead of writing, I'm doodling, sketching the view of Mt. Etna across the curve of the bay below the city, thinking of Paolo skiing on the other side.

A couple wanders by, stops, and admires my sketching.

"You're American?" they ask.

"Yes," I say, "but my grandmother was Italian."

"From Sicily?"

"No," I admit, "but my friend, who is skiing," I point to Etna, "his nonna was from Sicily."

I discover they are brother and sister, Filippo and Chiara Pandiani, with family roots both in Turin, in northwest Italy at the foot of the Alps, and also in Sicily. They are also winemakers and are checking on their Sicilian vineyards. I am struck by the fact that their Pandiani name sounds very familiar, and I think to myself, "In this life there are no coincidences."

Filippo and Chiara ask me a few questions about my visit here, and an amiable conversation ensues. My passionate appreciation of "things Italian," especially Italian wine, sparks interest in the three of us to continue our conversation in a more comfortable location.

Chiara suggests enjoying the view from the terrace of the Grand Hotel Timeo, just below the amphitheater. "It's especially lovely at sunset," she says, "with an aperitivo or glass of a wine." I readily agree and decide that Paolo can join us when he gets back from the slopes. I give Paolo a quick call; without the slightest hesitation, he agrees. Happily, he should join us there just before sunset.

It's a leisurely stroll down the winding, sloping pathway from the amphitheater to the hotel. Once on the terrace, we order cocktails. I turn to Filippo and Chiara and ask them about their wine. "I think I had your Nero d'Avola with lunch today, Antica Cantina Pandiani?"

"Yes," they answer, almost in unison. "That is our wine."

Filippo begins, "Let me tell you about the wine you drank." He continues, clearly warming up to telling their story. "Antica Cantina Pandiani Nero d'Avola—its story begins in the mists of time and mythology. It's a story of gods and Greeks, of Popes and the Italian royal family, truly a wine of 'ancient cellars.' It also spans Italy from north to south.

"Did you know," he asks, "that, according to legend, Dionysus or Bacchus, the god of wine, planted the first vineyard here on the island of Sicily at Naxos, just below Taormina?" He continues on without waiting for a response. "Perhaps that is why southern Italy has been producing wine for over four thousand years. The wine business here was already booming in 2000 BC when the Phoenicians arrived, and the Greeks called southern Italy 'The Land of Wine' when they settled in the region in the eighth century BC. The black-skinned Nero d'Avola may have been growing on the island even then."

Filippo pauses, as if to consider this history, and takes a sip of his drink. We all look out over the bay, a tiny plume of smoke now visible rising from the snow-capped peak of Mt. Etna. The sun is slipping toward the horizon as

Paolo arrives. He has picked up his drink at the hotel bar and found us on the terrace. Introductions are made.

"Did you see all the photos in the bar?" Paolo asks. "Seems we are in the company of the literati and glitterati—Truman Capote, Oscar Wilde, Greta Garbo, Clark Gable, D. H. Lawrence, Federico Fellini, Elizabeth Taylor..." We nod.

We watch as the sky transforms from subtle shades of blue to fiery orange and red. Mt Etna's snows and steamy plume take on an ethereal pink glow. The colors finally begin to fade to purple, and lights come on in the town and around the bay, like stars. Parts of Taormina glow golden as the sky darkens. We sit in an almost reverent silence, absorbing the beauty of the sight before us. Then, as if prompted by some invisible cue, without comment, we raise our glasses in unison to toast Bacchus and the vines he planted here. The clink of our four glasses is the only sound. It hangs in the air for a second or two as we each take a sip and then break into laughter at the ironic synchronicity of this magical moment.

We finally regain our composure, and Filippo resumes his story. "The wines of Sicily have been sought after and renowned for thousands of years—for example, Paul IV, an eleventh-century pope, loved Sicilian wines and brought them to Rome. In the 1500s, the pope's physician, Andrea Bacci, who was also a botanist, wrote a treatise on wines, *De Naturali Vinorum Historia*. Much of it is dedicated to Sicilian wines, of which he wrote, 'The vines grow prolifically, and as tall as men, so rich in grapes that ten plants are enough to render a bottle. The red wine is very strong, rich in fragrance and flavor, and it is optimal for long-term preservation.' That would be an apt description even today for a wine like Pandiani Nero d'Avola.

"Then, in 1713, Sicily came under the rule of the king of Italy, Victor Amedeus II. He sent members of his royal court to Sicily to select wines. Among these representatives were two Pandiani brothers, Piero and Antonio. Wine from Sicily, probably including Nero d'Avola, graced the cellars and tables of the royal court and the Pandiani family."

Chiara sighs and smiles. "Would you like to join us for dinner? We know a wonderful little restaurant." I consult briefly with Paolo, and we agree to meet them a little later in the evening.

**DESCRIPTION:** Nero d'Avola ("Black from Avola" in Italian) is "the most important red wine grape in Sicily" and is one of Italy's most important indigenous varieties. It is named after Avola, near Syracusa in the southeast of Sicily.

This earthy Old World varietal seems to produce wines that are capable of calling one back to an earlier time and atmosphere—filtered with afternoon sunlight and redolent with the smells of fresh, strong coffee; sea breezes and newly plowed fields; and someone's grandmother's cooking wafting from an open cottage window just down the cobblestone street.

Antica Cantina Pandiani Nero d'Avola is made in the traditional style, carefully crafted and fermented. It is not aged in oak, so all the flavors of the grape can be appreciated. The wine is dark and nicely acidic, with sweet, soft tannins and plum or prune fruit and sometimes peppery flavors. It is often compared to New World Shiraz.

Best served at sixty to sixty-four degrees Fahrenheit and allowed some time to open and breathe.

**TASTING NOTES:** Pandiani Nero d'Avola pours into your glass a dark and intense ruby red. As you swirl it and raise it to your nose, the wine offers lush aromas of dark berries and cherries, and a hint of herbs, pepper, and anise spice.

Unoaked, this is a medium-bodied wine, nicely fresh, with soft tannins and refreshing and food-complementing acidity. It has considerable character and is velvety and graceful.

Sip, savoring it slowly. You'll detect tastes of plum, black cherries, and berries, perhaps some blueberry, as well as licorice and a hint of pepper. The finish is long and persistent.

**FOOD PAIRINGS:** If you thought Nero de Avola was a wine to have only with pizza or pasta, you might be mistaken. This is also a Sicilian steak wine; dark and complex—every taste lingers and develops.

Of course, it was meant to accompany with Mediterranean fare and is especially good with roasted or grilled lamb, other grilled meats, shish kebabs, or ribs.

To be transported to Sicily, try this with the versatile caponata, the eggplant, caper and olive-based Sicilian salad sometimes spiked with sweet peppers or artichokes. Caponata also makes the perfect topping for grilled tuna and salmon.

# Fiano

## The Wine of the Bees—Inspired by Antica Cantina Pandiani Fiano

**STORY:** The restaurant is tucked neatly away, down a tiny alley well off the main street of Taormina. There are tiny lights, arrayed like stars, all over the ceiling, and candles everywhere. The scents coming from the kitchen promise a wonderful meal.

Filippo and Chiara greet us warmly. "We know the owner and chef here well—she still uses her grandmother's recipes," he says. "Let's see what she has for us tonight." A lovely white-haired woman emerges from the kitchen, as if on cue, carrying a bottle of white wine.

"May I pour you all a glass?" she asks, looking at Filippo and smiling. Filippo nods.

"I took the liberty of asking Rosa to bring out a bottle of our Fiano. I think it will go well with dinner," Filippo explains. Paolo and I lift our glasses and inhale deeply. We smell summer—sensuous honeysuckle and warm summer fruits. The taste is of ripe peaches and citrus, honey and almonds. Paolo smiles.

We decide to share a number of dishes. It will be a long evening of good food, good wine, and good conversation when we are not eating and drinking! Our dinner includes tuna carpaccio; simple grilled sardines splashed with lemon; *insalata di mare*, a salad of seafood tossed with olive oil, lemon, and herbs; stuffed artichokes; spaghetti with *ricci di mare* (sea urchins' roe), which is heavenly; *pasta alla Norma*; *involtini di pesce spada* (grilled swordfish rolls); and *grigliata mista,* a mixed seafood grill.

As she places our primo courses on the table, Rosa shares the poetic imagery that links *pasta alla Norma* to Mt Etna: the tomatoes are lava; the aubergines, cinders; the basil, leafy greenery; the ricotta, snow. "My nonna told me this," she says. And so Sicily's timeless recipes live on.

With our encouragement, Filippo tells us more about their family history, and also about the Fiano we are drinking. I have to admit, he is quite a good storyteller.

"The year was 1714. Piero and Antonio Pandiani have been sent from Turin, in northern Italy, by the king of Italy, to select and bring back wines for the royal court from the newly acquired province of Sicily, famous for its wines.

"The brothers spend several months in Sicily. The wines, they find, are indeed worthy to be served at the royal court. There are many different varieties, made from grape varieties not found in the north. The flavors are different from what they are used to—full, luscious, rich—capturing the essence of the island—the fire of the mighty Mount Etna, the sensuous warmth of the sun, the freshness of the sea breezes."

"Yes," I think, "that is a perfect description of the wine."

Filippo continues, "Antonio finds something else in Sicily, too—the beautiful Francesca. Her family is Sicilian aristocracy, and she is as talented as she is beautiful, in both music and poetry. Antonio is enchanted and delighted when her family approves his marriage proposal. She will come back with him to Turin.

"I can picture them, even today, as I walk through our vineyards here. Sometimes I even think I feel them walking beside me and hear them softly talking, as lovers do." Filippo gets a dreamy look in his eyes, as if remembering this waking dream.

"As they are walking through her family's vineyards, Francesca stops and pulls Antonio close. 'You must promise me that you will bring some of my favorite wine to your home, to our new home,' Francesca says. 'Here, from these grapes. See how the bees love them? They were called *apiana* by the Romans, but today we call them *fiano*. I love the wine from these grapes. And though I love you, I will need some of the sun and the warmth, and the scents and the tastes of my Sicily in my new home in the far north.' Antonio seals his promise with a kiss."

To illustrate, Filippo proffers Chiara a kiss, dramatically stroking her cheek, skillfully recreating for us this historical tender moment. With continued flare, as if rehearsed, Filippo and Chiara raise their glasses. "To love. And to our Fiano."

"We honor our history on our label," says Chiara. "Antica Cantina Pandiani—the ancient cellar of Pandiani. Sometimes I wonder if perhaps this Fiano was reserved solely for the pleasure of Francesca and the House of Pandiani, or if it also found its way onto the tables of the royal court there in Turin. The answer may be lost in history, but as Antonio and Francesca's descendants, we are fortunate to still enjoy it today."

Rosa reappears with dessert: little white cakes topped with a candied cherry. *"Minni di virgini,* virgins' breasts," says Chiara. "They were created to remember and celebrate Saint Agatha, the patron saint of Catania, a city about fifty kilometers south of Taormina."

I must have looked puzzled.

Chiara continues, "Agatha was a beautiful young woman of Catania who had converted to Christianity and taken a vow of chastity. However, the pagan Roman governor of Sicily lusted for her. When Agatha rebuffed his amorous advances, he retaliated by ordering her breasts pulled off. Then he roasted her in a kiln for good measure. She died on February 5, 251. These little cakes symbolize, to me at least, what Sicily is all about—an epicurean isle brimming with black humor, where every pain morphs into pleasure."

**DESCRIPTION:** Although it is one of the oldest "classic" grapes of Italy, today Fiano is one of Italy's great undiscovered grape varieties. With the Sicilian ability to produce great white wines, this makes for a stunning wine—a gem waiting to be discovered.

The Pandiani Estate replanted Fiano grapes in their Sicilian vineyard about ten years ago. Today, these vines are producing a lovely example of classic Fiano, which has been described as "racy, yet delicate." This might describe a Thoroughbred or Arabian horse, or an exciting woman, or an intriguing wine...

This Fiano has substantial body for a white wine and is very flavorful, with good structure, texture, and acidity. It is definitely ready to enjoy now, but a few years' aging will allow it to develop lovely additional complexity.

I recommend you serve it chilled to forty-five to fifty degrees Fahrenheit—not too cold, to allow all its beautiful bouquet and flavors to shine through.

**TASTING NOTES:** Antica Cantina Pandiani Fiano shimmers a pale straw yellow in your glass. Appealing aromas of summer fruits and flowers rise as you swirl the glass—luscious, ripe pears and peaches, fresh citrus, sensuous honeysuckle.

This is a substantial, medium-bodied white wine, fresh yet intriguingly complex on the palate. Savor the peach and pear flavors, the refreshing lemon-citrus notes, and the elegant overtones of honey, almond, and hazelnut. These are balanced by some herbaceousness, good minerality, and a crisp acidity. The finish is long and fresh.

Enjoyed now, in its "youth," the fruity, floral, and honey flavors predominate; with a few years aging, the wine becomes more complex, and the nutty, spicy notes become slightly more pronounced.

**FOOD PAIRINGS:** Fiano's racy acidity makes it perfect for foods with high fat content, such as triple-creme cheeses, salami, and sausages, and it can be used to add acidity and a wealth of flavor to a wine-friendly salad dressing.

In Sicily, this is the wine of choice for the sardine harvest—If you can find them here, grab some fresh sardines, grill them, and then crack open a bottle of this Fiano. Pure, unadulterated delight, and a virtual trip to this island of fire and sun.

Tired of beer with fish and chips? Does your girlfriend prefer wine with her fish and chips? This Fiano is perfect—try it, and you may never go back to beer!

Of course, Fiano will complement many seafood preparations—from tuna or salmon carpaccio to grilled, baked, or fried fish of almost any type, as well as seafood soups, stews, and pastas.

Fiano pairs beautifully with lemon and garlic chicken, or chicken saltimbocca—chicken thigh meat, pounded thin, stuffed with goat cheese and fresh tarragon, and wrapped in *prosciutto* and baked—and also many veal or pork dishes.

Fiano is also one white wine that goes well with many dishes normally associated with red wines, such as stuffed eggplant and pasta alla Norma.

# Anglianico
## Court Intrigue—Inspired by Antica Cantina Pandiani Aglianico

**STORY:** Paolo has persuaded Filippo to join him for a few hours of skiing on nearby Mt. Etna. Chiara and I decline, opting for spa treatments, shopping, and lunch, not necessarily in that order. I discover Filippo is not the only storyteller in the family.

"It's a family secret," Chiara said, taking another sip of her Pandiani Aglianico. "It's also the story of this wine, and it explains why a family from northern Italy has its name on a red wine from southern Italy, from Sicily. Filippo would never tell you, but the Pandiani family has some royal blood flowing in its veins. Let me explain..." She swirls her glass and looks deeply into the dark wine.

"The story of Aglianico begins in the mists of time, with the ancient Greeks. And as Filiipo described the other night, the story of the Pandianis spans Italy from north to south. The Pandiani family is from Turin, the home of the Italian royal family, the House of Savoy, the world's oldest and longest-reigning dynasty. The Pandianis were members of the court of Turin—but I'm getting ahead of my story.

"When the Greeks began to settle in southern Italy and Sicily in the eighth century BC, they brought wine-making with them, planting several varieties of grapes, including the black-skinned red grape that has come to be known as Aglianico. The origins of the name are now lost to history, although one theory is that it is derived from the Latin word for Greece, *Hellenica*.

"The wines of Sicily, of course, have been renowned for thousands of years, and sought after by popes, dukes, and kings. They came to be associated with the House of Savoy and Turin when, in 1713, the Treaty of Utrecht rewarded Vittorio Amedeo II, Duke of Savoy, new lands and the Crown of Sicily. He was now a king.

"As Filippo told, our family history says Vittorio sent a member of the Pandiani family, Piero, known for his taste in wine, to Sicily to select and oversee bringing wines back to the royal court. Piero took his younger brother

Antonio with him. One can imagine that the royal family was delighted to now enjoy the same exceptional wines as the pope, these southern Italian wines so different from those of northern Italy—'the sunlight of Sicily and the fires of Mt. Etna,' captured in a bottle—deep dark red, warm, intense, and smooth. And so the Pandiani family not only enjoyed the wines of Sicily at court dinners, they had some in their own cellars as well."

I nod, remembering Filippo's story.

Chiara continues, "But that's not the secret…you know how royal courts were in those days—full of intrigue. King Vittorio, it seems, was enchanted by the new member of the Pandiani household, the lovely young lady Francesca from Palermo, married to Piero's younger brother, Antonio. We're told she was a gifted writer of poetry. I can imagine her entertaining the royal court at salons, as was the custom in those days, with readings, and perhaps even having private audiences with the king.

"And if the king asked for private poetry readings from Francesca, surely she would have obliged. Did Vittorio and Francesca share more than wine and poetry? You know the sensuous nature of Italians." Chiara smiles knowingly.

"We think it's very possible Vittorio and Francesca were lovers. Of course, she would have concealed that from Antonio, or if he suspected, he would not have admitted it. Antonio and Francesca had ten children. The secret oral history passed down through the generations of Pandiani women says at least one of the sons was of royal blood."

"So it's only fitting," I say, nodding, "that you carry on this tradition—the marriage of north and south—Aglianico wine from Sicily produced under the name of a family of the royal court of Turin."

Who knows what the afternoon will bring, besides a luxuriously relaxing spa treatment? And then there's the evening.

**DESCRIPTION:** Originally from Greece and an early Roman favorite, the Aglianico grape was planted as early as the seventh century BC in southern Italy. Since the Aglianico vine prefers dry, warm conditions, it was introduced to Sicily from the Basilicata area on the mainland, with outstanding results.

Pandiani Aglianico is produced in southeastern Sicily, near the "Valley of the Temples" and the ancient town of Agrigento, founded as Akragas around 582 BC, which the Greek poet Pindar described as "the most beautiful city of the mortals."

It is made using only steel tanks, which preserves the fruity bouquet and the purity of the flavors of the Aglianico grapes, and then aged for six months in the bottle. Ready to enjoy twelve to twenty-four months after vintage, this is a remarkable and easy-to-enjoy wine.

**TASTING NOTES:** This dark red wine has a remarkable bouquet of dark wild berries. The flavor is smooth and luscious—dark berries and cherries, with spicy black currant, exotic spice, and licorice notes, and hints of chocolate and plums. Pandiani Aglianico is a stylish, intriguing young red, with fine tannins and a ripe, balanced finish, complex and structured. It can be enjoyed a mere half hour after opening.

**FOOD PAIRINGS:** Pandiani Aglianico is the perfect wine to serve with Mediterranean dishes and the cuisine of the island of sunlight and fire—pasta, veal or lamb, and of course seafood, such as "zuppe di pesce," a fish-and-tomato stew, or perhaps its San Francisco cousin, cioppino.

For a wonderful vegetarian meal, pair Pandiani Aglianico with eggplant parmigiana and spaghetti with garlic and olive oil, or perhaps *pasta alla Norma* (spaghetti with sautéed tomato, eggplant, and ricotta), named in honor of the Sicilian composer Vincenzo Bellini and his opera *Norma*. Eggplant is a staple of Sicilian cuisine, introduced by the Arabs. Almost any rich eggplant dish is wonderful with this Anglianico. Try it with a Persian-style eggplant stew—sauté onion; add lamb chunks, garlic, and some turmeric, stirring until the lamb begins to brown. Add tomato sauce or crushed tomatoes, and simmer for about two and a half hours. Then prepare eggplant—peel and cut into slices or chunks. Sauté the eggplant in oil over medium heat until just starting to brown, add to the lamb and tomato, and simmer for about another hour. Serve over basmati rice or with bread. Melt-in-your-mouth luscious!

And of course, Sicilian pizza is not enjoyed to the fullest without a glass or two of a fine Sicilian wine, especially an Aglianico.

# Region: Trentino — Alto Adige/Südtirol

**Wines:**
    Chardonnay
    Pinot Bianco White Blend

**Wineries:**
    Volano
    L'Arco

# Trentino—Alto Adige/Südtirol

---

SURROUNDED BY THE Alps and Dolomites, towering limestone saw-toothed mountains, and bordering Austria and Switzerland, this is the northernmost region in Italy.

Historically two separate regions, Trentino and Alto Adige were combined into one for political purposes. At the start of the nineteenth century, both of these areas were ruled by the Austrians. Alto Adige had been a part of Austria's Tyrol for hundreds of years. It is also known as the Suditrol (or South Tyrol). Trentino, just to the south, was originally Italian but was conquered and ruled by the Austrians. In 1919, after the defeat of the Austrians in World War I, the lands were annexed by Italy. Since this time, they have been one political region, each "province" having much local autonomy. However, due to this history, the culture and foods of the area have strong Austrian and Germanic influences, uniquely and quite pleasurably blended over this past century with the Italian flavors and traditions.

The area is mountainous with only about 15 percent of the land being arable. Corn grows in the south, in Trentino, and polenta is a staple there. The region grows a wide range of grape varieties, many not seen in other parts of Italy, in part due to the climate and in part to the Austrian-German heritage.

Alto Adige is renowned for minerally, well-structured white wines, with white grape varieties grown in more than 55 percent of the region's vineyards. International varieties like Pinot Grigio, Chardonnay, Pinot Blanc (Pinot Bianco), and Sauvignon Blanc thrive in cool-climate vineyards.

Trentino is known for several native grapes, as well as cultivation of international varieties. Trentino produces several red wines, the sweet "Vino Sancto," and some very good whites. Native varieties include Nosiola, Terolego, and Marzemino; international grape varieties include Chardonnay, Pinot Grigio, Pinot Nero, Merlot, Cabernet, and Muller-Thurgau.

# Chardonnay
# A Ferrari Goes to France, or the Demise
# of the ABC Club—Inspired by Volano
# Chardonnay

**STORY:** It was the year before I went to Italy.

Matt and Kate had just returned from several weeks in France and Italy—their dream vacation, and belated honeymoon. They invited me, Giotto, and a couple of other friends over to catch up on news and to share wine and food from the areas they visited. All of us were looking forward to hearing more details and seeing more pictures of their travels. First, they spent a week on a luxurious canal barge, plying the canals and visiting villages in the beautiful Burgundy wine region of France. The cruise was total relaxation and romance, with a focus on wine, food, and chocolate! From there, they went to northern Italy, to stunning Lake Como with beautiful villas perched above sparkling waters, then on to the Italian Alps and Trentino with quant villages and acres of vineyards, and finally Venice and the lovely seacoast to the west of that enchanting city. Romantic, adventurous, sensual.

Did I mention that it was summer? Lighter fare? And white wines? And that most of us belong to that heretical club (at least in California): "ABC"— "Anything but Chardonnay"? Do you wonder why our ABC Club came to be? I think Kate summed it up best. As Kate says, "I love drinking wine and tasting the flavors of the grapes. I just don't like sucking on an oak board or drinking burnt caramel."

And yet, a fundamental attitudinal and preferential shift occurred, quite by accident, at the very beginning of their honeymoon travels in France. Their story may surprise you.

"It was a revelation," said Matt. "There we were, in the beautiful little French village of Chablis, tasting the wines that bear the name of the area. We'd also had a Chablis with dinner the previous evening and were rather enchanted by these Chablis wines—a lovely pale greenish-yellow color, star-bright clarity, and a racy green-apple acidity. Some of them had a distinctive 'flinty' or 'steely' character, which the French describe as *'goût de pierre à fusil'* ('tasting of gunflint'). I'm embarrassed to report I asked about the grapes and was equally embarrassed—and somewhat amazed—to learn Chablis is made from one hundred percent Chardonnay grapes! Our wine expert explained that Chablis is one of the 'purest' expressions of the varietal character of Chardonnay due to the simple style of wine making in the region—most is neither fermented nor aged in oak.

"And then we went to Italy...I know, you're thinking Soave and Pinot Grigio. But we discovered Italy also produces Chardonnay—very good Chardonnay. And most of it is made in the style of French Chablis, that is to say, unoaked. At a beautiful little winery in northeast of Italy, not far from the Italian Alps, we learned that Chardonnay vines were brought to Italy in the late 1800s, and to northern Italy in particular around 1900 by Guilio Ferrari, who had studied wine making in France. He wanted to make Champagne-style sparkling wines, and also still white wine, in the French manner. He thought the Chardonnay grape would do well in his native region of Trentino, in the foothills of the Italian Alps, since the cooler weather and soil were much like the Chablis and Champagne regions of France. And so, our white wine of choice in Italy became unoaked Chardonnay." He chuckled. "Does this mean we're not members of the ABC Club anymore?"

We look around, and soon we are chuckling, too. We'd been listening, talking, and admiring photos, all while sipping a fresh, crisp white wine. Its taste was citrus-apple-melon, with a nice minerally overtone, beautifully complementing the oysters, salad with beets and goat cheese, vichyssoise, and seafood pasta we'd been enjoying. And just what was this wine? We checked the label again—it was a lovely unoaked Italian Chardonnay, bottled under the Volano label, from the Trentino region. Perhaps we would change the name of our club to "ABOC"—Anything But Oaked Chardonnay, now that we knew how good a Chardonnay could be.

**DESCRIPTION:** The Chardonnay grape was introduced to Italy in the nineteenth century. While this aristocratic Burgundian white grape is planted throughout Italy, it especially thrives in the northeast regions of Fruili, Trentino, and Veneto, the home of the Volano winery that creates this lovely unoaked wine. As it is cold-fermented and aged in stainless-steel tanks, one can taste the true varietal character of the grape, without the influence or interference of wood.

This could be the perfect wine for those who don't want sweet Chardonnay or weak Chardonnay or a Chardonnay with (*egads*) oak.

Recently, at Italy's most important wine fair, *VinItaly*, held each spring in Verona, Volano Chardonnay captured the hearts of the connoisseurs of good wines, and won several awards—another love story in Verona.

Serve this refreshing white wine well chilled, at a temperature of forty-seven to fifty degrees Fahrenheit, in tulip-shaped wine glasses to enjoy it to the fullest.

**TASTING NOTES:** The color of this lovely, fresh Volano Chardonnay is that of pale straw—barely yellow, perhaps a hint of green, as it sparkles, star-bright, in your glass. Swirl. As you hold it to your nose, the perfume is fruity and distinctive—refreshing green apples, some citrus, perhaps melon. The taste is crisp, inviting, and dry, with a clean finish.

Like the bouquet, the taste is of crisp apples, citrus fruits, some melon overtones, and even a hint of sandalwood. You may also taste the essence of the limestone in the soil—a slight echo of the sea that makes this wine so perfect an accompaniment to oysters in particular and seafood in general. Unoaked and unfettered, the simple purity of the Chardonnay grape shines through.

**FOOD PAIRINGS:** There are some who claim that Chardonnay is surprisingly hard to pair with food, but this unoaked gem of a white wine makes food pairing decisions simple. Volano Chardonnay is a great complement to seafood, chicken, and salad, as well as pastas and risottos.

Volano Chardonnay is also ideal all by itself as an aperitif before a meal. For something different in a before-dinner drink, use it to make kir, a French cocktail made with crème de cassis (black-currant liquor) topped with a fresh, fruit-forward, slightly minerally unoaked white wine. It was originally made in France with Chablis. Since Volano Chardonnay has all these characteristics, it will make a perfect kir in the classic French tradition. The recipe is one-tenth to one-fifth creme de cassis, nine-tenths to four-fifths white wine.

Try this unoaked Chardonnay with Vichyssoise (fancy French for cold leek and potato soup) and a nice tossed green salad on a hot summer evening.

This Chardonnay is simply awesome with fresh, raw oysters or tuna carpaccio. It's lovely with sole, white-truffle risotto, linguine with clam sauce, shrimp scampi, or even a hearty seafood lasagna.

And you'll probably be surprised how well it works with guacamole and grilled shrimp. Try it with tempura! And it goes quite nicely with many curry dishes, too.

# *Pinot Bianco Blend*
## *The Best of Both Worlds — Inspired by L'Arco Bianco DOC Alto Adige*

**STORY:** You could be forgiven for thinking you are in Bavaria, or Austria, in the Alps. For indeed, the Dolomites and the Alps rise here in all their magnificent snow-covered glory, providing beautiful backdrops for picture-postcard valley villages, fairy-tale castles, and some superb skiing.

The street signs are in German and Italian. You hear German spoken almost as often as Italian. And knodel, potato dumplings, so characteristically German, are perhaps more prevalent on menus here than spaghetti.

Towns and villages are known by both their German and Italian names. Nestled in the northern part of Italy, this area, known as the "Alto Adige" or "*Südtirol*," was part of the Austro-Hungarian Empire until just after World War I. Famous for wines since the fifth century BC, the warm days and cool nights are perfect for grape cultivation. Wines from Alto Adige are best described as "mountain wines"—vineyard sites range from six hundred feet to a dizzying thirty-three hundred feet above sea level. And indeed, the village of Tramin (or Termeno) is the home of the grape Gewurtztraminer.

You may ask, "What would it be like to visit Alto Adige in the winter?" Well, the skiing is superb, as is the snowboarding. And you would enjoy many memorable evenings in beautiful lodges, or in picturesque and lively village taverns, sitting around a warm, inviting fire with good friends and good food—what could be better?

Or perhaps you would prefer visiting in the spring, when the hillsides bloom with alpine flowers?

Summer, on the other hand, is the season for hiking and trekking into the Alps, perhaps along the Sentiero della Pace (the Path of Peace). This historic trail was created and dedicated in memory of the First World War; it brings you unspoiled nature at its best.

In the fall, the apples for which this region is famous ripen, along with the grapes, providing a unique combination of colors and scents.

So without doubt, the Alto Adige offers year-round pleasures, complemented and accentuated by the foods and wines produced and served in the region. Every season offers a singularly unique experience, the excellent food and wine there being the unchanging thread that ties these memorable experiences together. Perhaps you'll decide on several visits to sample the pleasures of the different seasons, as I did.

If you want to visit both the Austrian or German Alps and Italy, this could be the perfect place, the best of both worlds.

I can't tell you which season is best. Paolo will of course tell you winter, avid skier that he is. Whenever you visit, we can tell you that you will not be disappointed. And you will love the food and wines—from knodel to speck (a succulent local ham) to pasta with cream sauce, best consumed with a great local white wine. We were delighted to discover one of our favorite Tuscan wineries, L'Arco, has vineyards here and makes a superb white blend they label simply as "Bianco." It is not just a wine for summer—it's delicious with these and many other foods at any time of year. Like the Alto Adige, a place for all seasons, this is a wine for all seasons.

**DESCRIPTION:** The owner of L'Arco winery had a vision—to produce a white version of the famed red "Super Tuscan" wine. After all, he was from Tuscany, and his L'Arco winery produces exceptional Tuscan wines, including a Super Tuscan. He found a vineyard in the Alto Adige, an area known for producing great white wines, and the rest, as they say, is history. L'Arco's Bianco is a blend of four grapes, creating a wine more complex and intriguing than each would be alone—truly a "Super White."

L'Arco Bianco is based on the classic Alto Adige white grape, Pinot Bianco, which is about 50 percent of the blend. Pinot Bianco is a mutation of Pinot Noir, with no pigment—a white version of Pinot Noir. Another local grape, Gewurztraminer, from the Alto Adige village of Tramin/Termeno, adds restrained spicy notes, with Chardonnay and Sauvignon Blanc adding their subtle charms and characteristics and rounding out the blend.

L'Arco Bianco is a masterwork of wine-making art. The vintner allows the wine to sit on the lees all winter, contributing complexity and blending flavors. It is then bottled and aged an additional three months.

This might be the consummate food wine for those who love a good white wine—it is fruity yet not overly so, freshly acidic yet not cutting or raw, subtly complex, and transparent. "It is a great example of a classic Italian wine," Paolo says, "that does not demand attention, but that rewards the level of attention you give it. Sort of like a lovely woman I know..."

**TASTING NOTES:** This L'Arco Bianco from Alto Adige is a beautiful straw yellow in color with golden overtones—summer sunlight captured in liquid form. It is complex and intense with notes of fresh fruit—green apple, pear, perhaps some soft citrus—accompanied by light hints of bread crust. It has a crisp, zippy acidity, which makes it a very food-friendly wine. Rich, fragrant, and very harmonious, there is a long, lingering, and fruit-filled finish.

**FOOD PAIRINGS:** In the Alto Adige, you would find this wine served as an aperitivo or with antipasti. It also accompanies such local specialties as "speck," or any similar succulent smoky cured ham, and knodel or canederli—potato dumplings, usually made with speck and spinach.

Pair this wine with chicken, especially chicken breasts, or any flaky white fish, perhaps in a simple sauce. We also like L'Arco Bianco with duck à l'orange. If you have a hunter in your life, try it with game birds, such as quail or pheasant.

Italians would recommend you serve this with grilled fresh sardines and light pasta dishes, such as fresh pasta with a simple yet elegant olive oil and garlic sauce.

We like it with sushi and Japanese cuisine, as well.

And a friend in the States swears by this L'Arco Bianco for picnics and barbeques, whether he's serving roast suckling pig, cold fried chicken with potato salad and coleslaw, or his famous Hawaiian BBQ chicken with pineapple, ginger, and soy sauce.

# Region: Lombardia

**Wines:**
   Chardonnay
   Cellatica (Barbera Red Blend)
   Franciacorta

**Wineries:**
   Cà del Vént

# Lombardia

LOMBARDIA, IN THE north of Italy, is bordered on the north by Switzerland and on the south by Lake Garda. The northern portions are mountainous; the Alps give way to piedmont and gently rolling foothills, which in turn flatten out to an alluvial plain in the south.

Lombardia is graced by a number of scenic lakes, primarily in the foothill zone. The most famous are Lakes Maggiore, Como, and Garda, but there are other smaller and equally beautiful ones that lie at the foot of the Alps.

The foothills zone is also home to a very distinctive wine area, known as Franciacorta, in the province of Brescia.

Lombardia, and particularly the province of Brescia, is also known for its cuisine. It's north of the "oil line," so many recipes use butter instead of olive oil. And while I love a wonderful, fresh, fruity olive oil, I also agree with Julia Child—"with enough butter, anything is good."

# *Chardonnay*
# *Aging Well—Inspired by Cà del Vént Ubiqua*
# *Chardonnay*

**STORY:** My introduction to Cà del Vént wines came the year before I went to Tuscany, and I was determined to visit this winery and sample more of its wine when I finally arrived in Italy. It's a small winery located in Lombardia, in the Franciacorta wine region in the province of Brescia. Let me tell you about that most memorable introduction.

Jean-Luc and Catherine were hosting a wine tasting, which was focused on older, aged wines. They are a delightful couple, French imports, tall, elegant, sophisticated, and fun. Despite being somewhere north of fifty, they look and act ten to fifteen years younger, even with the gray hair they both proudly wear. We never thought of them as older, just more experienced. Perhaps it's the dancing, lucky genetics, their French lifestyle (food and wine), or their attitude toward life that keeps them so vibrant. They introduced many of us to ballroom dancing as well; some of us have fallen in love with the Viennese waltz and the foxtrot, too.

Jean-Luc smiles and says, "I have a surprise, something very different, for you tonight. If conditions and circumstances are favorable, wines, like people, develop complexity as they mature, and it is complexity that distinguishes a good wine from a great wine. The notion of cellaring wines for many years to obtain as much potential depth and complexity as possible is primarily associated with reds and fortified wines, such as vintage port. However, the process can be applied to whites as well. Some white wines, that is. The two most well-known, and famous, examples are the prestige cuvee champagnes, such as Cristal, and Chardonnay from Montrachet, both from France. These can range in price from several hundred to almost one thousand dollars a bottle.

"On our last trip to the continent, Catherine and I visited northeastern Italy, the area around Brescia, known for its luxury foods, such as white truffles, and also wonderful wines. We found a small boutique vineyard, Cà del Vént, which sits high on a hill. There we tasted a ten- to twelve-year-old Chardonnay, 'Ubiqua,' made from very ripe grapes. This gives the wine a slightly higher alcohol content, as well as great depth of flavor and complexity. It's much more affordable than the Montrachet, and equally intriguing. We think of it as a ballroom dancer of a wine—powerful yet graceful and elegant. We'd like to share it with you tonight. We've let it breathe, and we advise you to drink it slowly to fully appreciate all its nuances of flavor."

I swirl the glass, inhale deeply, and then take a sip. There are so many layers of aroma and flavor—floral, a variety of fruit, and deep spice notes. This is a serious Chardonnay, potent and a deep golden color in the glass. Aging has truly transformed this wine.

We all agree; it transcends our notion of Chardonnay and is unlike any other wine made from this varietal we have ever tasted. Intensely rich, it is perfectly balanced and stunning in every way, truly memorable. Jean-Luc's comparison is apt—the wine's flavors truly dance across the palate, slowly, easily, yet powerfully. This may be an Italian wine, but as I reverently sip it, I swear I can hear a Viennese waltz.

Later, I thank Jean-Luc for this memorable experience and for providing the subject for my next wine blog—"Yes, Virginia, there are some white wines that improve with age" is how I think I will start it. This being the holiday season, I can't resist doing a takeoff on the 1897 *NY Sun* editorial "Is There a Santa Claus?" that has become an indelible part of American Christmas folklore, which began with the famous reply, "Yes, Virginia, there is a Santa Claus."

If you're looking for an amazing and unique white wine for a special dining occasion to pair with rich and luxurious foods, try this Cà del Vént Ubiqua Chardonnay. Magnifique! Or, "Magnifico!"

**DESCRIPTION:** Cà del Vént Ubiqua Chardonnay is a unique and memorable wine, elegant, balanced, and powerful. The Cà del Vént winery and vineyard sits on a windswept hill in northeastern Italy, near Lake Iseo and the foothills of the Italian Alps. The scenery is as spectacular as the wine.

The vines are hand-tended, and the grapes are hand-harvested and carefully selected for this very special wine. The vintner selects slightly overripe grapes, which results in a wine with a slightly higher alcohol percentage (14 percent), as well as a wine of great complexity, body, flavor, and ability to age magnificently. Made with 100 percent Chardonnay, Cà del Vént Ubiqua is aged eighteen months in new oak and then seven years in the bottle before release, which produces an intense richness. It is also slightly oxidized, like a fine sherry, which contributes to the golden color as well as the notes of butterscotch on the palate.

This fine chardonnay is named after a beautiful and symbolic piece of sculpture by Mario Diacono designed especially for the vineyard grounds. The work of art is composed of three marble cubes—black (in a pond), white (on a hill), and red (suspended above the earth in a tree). This symbolizes transformation through space and also time—much as grapes are transformed into wine by the actions of the vintner and the fullness of time—most appropriate for this wine, a truly transformed Chardonnay, and truly a work of art.

**TASTING NOTES:** Everything about this wine says "sumptuous and sophisticated." Chill nicely, and pour it into an elegant crystal goblet—this wine and you deserve it! The color is intense, deep yellow with golden highlights. Swirl, and savor the rich bouquet, a Strauss orchestra of scents—floral notes, ripe fruits (apricot, banana, pineapple, orange, and candied fruit), spice (vanilla and nutmeg), and a hint of coconut. The complex aroma carries over to the taste. Ubiqua is broad and powerful on the palate, yet definitely elegant, dry, and balanced. It is full of flavor, creamy, with complex fruit, spice, and butterscotch flavors. Let it waltz, slowly and gracefully, across your tongue and into your heart and memory.

**FOOD PAIRING:** This rich wine pairs well with similarly luxurious foods. Try it with foie gras, duck à l'orange, almost any dish with those sinfully delicious and extravagant white truffles from Brescia, such as a white-truffle risotto, or lobster or oysters. For a dessert course, it will complement an elegant fruit-and-cheese assortment—Cà del Vént Ubiqua Chardonnay is especially nice with fruits such as pears, apples, and grapes; goat cheese, brie or camembert, blue-cheese-stuffed olives, and maybe curls of a good parmigiano-reggiano, a manchego, or an aged gouda.

# Cellatica

## Me and Edith and George—Inspired by Cà del Vént Cellatica

**STORY:** I'm sharing this with you because, well, you're a friend. And friends share the best things, the little hidden gems they find, that are too good not to be shared.

The Italian Lakes region is rightfully famous, and its lakes are considered by many to be the loveliest in the world. Everyone from Pliny the Younger to Ernest Hemingway has written about Lake Maggiore, Lake Garda, and everyone's favorite, Lake Como. Backdropped by the Alps, with a milder climate that gives them a more southern feel, with lemon, pomegranate, and even palm trees, and quaint villages and resort towns, these lakes are high on the list of must-visit places in Italy.

Well, it may surprise you when I say I found another lake, even more enchanting, but less well-known by tourists. And all because of a paper I wrote for an English class in college.

The assignment: a paper on a Pulitzer Prize–winning author, for an American twentiety-century literature class. I chose the first woman winner of the Pulitzer Prize for a Novel, Edith Wharton. She won the Pulitzer in 1921, just five years after the Prize was established, for *The Age of Innocence.* In addition to twenty-two novels, she wrote eighty-five short stories, three books of poetry, and, I discovered, six travel books on France and Italy. In reading some of these, I saw Italy through Edith's eyes and heart. One of her favorite places, Lake Iseo, is described in her short story, *The Confessional,* as "the blue lake far below, hidden in its hills like a happy secret in a stern heart…[the great lakes] are like the show pictures that some nobleman hangs in his public gallery; but our Iseo is the treasure that he hides in his inner chamber." I was intrigued.

In planning my "writer's holiday" trip to Lake Iseo, I learned other literary figures had also been enchanted by the area and spent considerable time there. Perhaps the most well-known is George Sand (the pen name of the French novelist Aurore Dupin). Aurore was known not only for her literary achievements in the mid-1800s but also for her scandalous conduct, dressing as a man, and her ten-year affair with Frederick Chopin. She wrote of Lake Iseo to a friend in London: "Come, I have found a lovely place to live."

When I visited, I found that Lake Iseo and the surrounding area offer many different things—a beautiful lake, clear blue; stunning villas and quaint villages terraced up the mountainsides or nesting along the lake shore, fishing boats tied up at water's edge; superb hiking; wonderful biking and several bike races during the year; festivals every month, including several devoted to the food and wines of the area, such as sardines, wild boar (called cinghiale), and spiedo, spit-roasted meat, as well as jazz and art; unique geologic formations, including the "Pyramids of Zone," rock pinnacle formations; and the largest island in any lake in all of Europe. Any of these things would be wonderful by themselves, but together, they make for a truly unique and magical place.

It was there, in a small café on a piazza overlooking the Lake and Monte Isolo, that large island, that I first tasted the red Cellatica wine, produced in hills around the small town of the same name, just to the east of the lake. Like Lake Iseo, Cellatica wine is an "undiscovered gem" that I hadn't heard of before I arrived here. And it's just as delightful, a blend of four grapes, smooth, easy to drink, good with almost any of the local foods, from antipasta, cheeses, and sardines, to pastas and roasted meats. And yes, of course, I even enjoyed it with pizza.

I'm sure Aurore/George and Chopin enjoyed a similar wine as they relaxed in her villa near Lovere, and that as a woman of excellent taste and sophistication, Edith Wharton did too. The scenery, the history, the culture, the food and wine—all inspiring, then and now.

I don't know if it will inspire me to achieve literary success, but I intend to keep drinking and serving Cellatica wine, like this delicious Cà del Vént Cellatica. Whenever I close my eyes and savor this wine, I am once again transported back to beautiful Lake Iseo.

**DESCRIPTION:** This Cà del Vént Cellatica truly exemplifies the old adage, "The whole is more than the sum of its parts."

Cellatica wine, named for the township in which it is produced, is a blend of four different grape varieties, the best known of which is Barbera (35 percent). The other grapes used are Marzemino (35 percent), Incrocio Terzi (15 percent), and Schiava Gentile (15 percent).

Cà del Vént (House of the Wind) exercises special care in the growing of its grapes, in vineyards high in the Campiani hills. The grapes are hand-harvested. Each of the four varietals that are blended to create this wine are vinified separately. This allows each grape to be harvested when it is at peak ripeness for the wine-making, and also keeps the character and flavor of each grape alive, both before and after blending of the individual wines to create this Cellatica. The wine ferments and ages for twelve months in steel tanks and then ages for another eighteen months in the bottle.

Because I find the painstaking care and centuries of wine-making skills applied to the creation of this wine so interesting, I think you'll be as fascinated as I was. Please let me tell you a little more about the grapes used in this blend.

You have probably heard of Barbera, but the other three may be less familiar to you. Barbera is perhaps the most widely grown grape in the Italian Piedmont and southern areas of Lombardy. It is a versatile grape, frequently used for blending for the structure and softness it adds. Barbara-based wines are ready to drink upon release and show a deep dark color, bright cherry flavors, smooth tannins, and structured, food-friendly acidity.

The Marzemino grape has been grown in the northern areas of Italy for hundreds of years. It's a diva—a temperamental, delicate grape, requiring attention and care and a long growing season. Wines produced from this grape have a characteristic dark tint and light plummy taste, bright acidity, with light hints of cherry and perhaps some almond flavors. If someone asked you to describe a typical Italian food wine, you'd probably come up with something that very closely resembled this. Wine made from the Marzemino grape was very popular and highly regarded in Austria in Mozart's day, which may explain the line in Mozart's opera *Don Giovanni*: "Versa il vino! Eccellente Marzemino!" ("Pour the wine! Excellent Marzemino!").

Incrocio Terzi was developed by Professor Luigi Manzoni of Italy's oldest school of oenology located in the town of Conegliano, in the Veneto region, in the 1930s. Incrocio Terzi is a cross of Cabernet Franc and Barbera.

Schiava Gentile is typically a blending grape, used for its fruity and mellowing characteristics.

These four grapes come together to make a persistent, soft, fine, and elegantly drinkable ruby-red wine that is at once delicately fruity, with a hint of spice, yet dry and well-balanced all the way through the finish.

As with most Barbera-based wines, this Cellatica is meant to be enjoyed now—no more aging required, although you could keep it in your cellar for another few years.

To enjoy it to its fullest, I recommend aerating to oxygenate using a decanter, letting it breathe for about an hour, and serving at sixty to sixty-seven degrees Fahrenheit.

**TASTING NOTES:** Cà del Vént Cellatica is a rich wine, an intense and deep ruby red with violet overtones.

Swirl it in your glass, admire the color, and then bring it to your nose—what will you discern in its complex aroma? Cherry brandy? Fruits and spices? A friend and wine connoisseur opined, "Hmm…lovely—and a little raw carpaccio, perhaps?"

And the taste—all the elements of each grape and the magical terroir of the Cà del Vént vineyards, contribute wonderful complexity to this elegant, full-bodied, and well-balanced wine. There is intense cherry fruit, with hints of plum and blackberry, and spiciness (some pepper, ginger, and perhaps curry) with elegant tannins and a nice acidity to balance most foods. It's smooth, with a lovely juicy bite, intense and persistent. Who knew an unoaked wine could be this good, this complex, yet so easy to drink?

**FOOD PAIRINGS:** This is a great, everyday drinking wine, and it goes well with most meals—you will certainly want to enjoy it with pizza or pasta.

This wine is definitely well matched with barbequed, grilled, roasted, or stewed meats and game; mushroom-based dishes, such as a hearty mushroom risotto; and well-aged or medium to softer cheeses.

Transport yourself to the province of Brescia, where Cellatica wine traditionally is served with cinghiale (wild boar), prepared in any number of delicious ways. And should you not find any wild boar in your local market, do try it with roast or grilled pork.

It's also served with spiedo (meat roasted slowly on a spit, usually for six to eight hours, so succulent it melts in your mouth) served with polenta (once thought to be an aphrodisiac), and also the Lombardy specialty pasta, *casoncelli*—ravioli filled with cheese, egg, bread crumbs, and sometimes beef.

Want something a little more robust than a white wine with those grilled sardines or smelt (or other full-flavored, slightly oily fish) to remind you of Lake Iseo? Try this Cellatica as a pairing—its fresh fruity taste, smooth tannins, and nice acidity complement the salty, oily sardines perfectly.

# The Best of Brescia—Inspired by Cà del Vént, Clavis Cellatica Superiore

**STORY:** Extraordinary…elegant…exquisite…extravagant…all these and more describe Cà del Vént Clavis Cellatica Superiore wine, deservedly a Gold Medal Winner at the 2011 London International Wine Challenge.

The essence of civilization and the heart of any culture can be found in its wine, its food, and its art. Some of the greatest examples of each can be found in northern Italy, in Lombardy, home of this amazing red wine, and all three come together in the story of Cà del Vént Clavis.

As I discovered on my visit to the Cà del Vént vineyard and winery, it is aptly named. It sits high atop a windswept hill in the foothills of the Italian Alps, just south of the beautiful Lake Iseo and north of Brescia. The scenery here is jaw-droppingly beautiful. Wine has been made here for over a thousand years, and in the tenth century it was so well regarded that it was exported to Milan and Rome. Even today, some of the most expensive and world-renowned wines are from this region of Italy. Cà del Vént Clavis is one of those, a brilliant example of the true art of wine-making.

And as I discovered on my visit, luxury is also the hallmark of the cuisine here. Consider these facts about the area around Brescia:

- The province boasts the greatest number of first-class restaurants cited in culinary guides for their high quality, elegance, and taste.
- Some of the best cheeses in Italy, such as Gran Padano and gorgonzola, are made here.
- It's the home of polenta, considered by some to be an aphrodisiac, as well as the perfect accompaniment to many Italian meat dishes, and which, like the "little black dress," can be dressed up or down to suit any culinary occasion from simple to sublime.
- The rare and treasured white truffle, which commands $3,000 to $6,000 a pound, grows in the forests of the surrounding hills. Unlike the French black truffle, these are almost always served raw, shaved

over pasta, egg dishes, or risotto, to preserve the delicate taste, which is considered one of the finest epicurean experiences on earth.

- Caviar has been produced here since Roman times, when Calvisius, a nobleman with exquisite tastes, moved here because of the indigenous sturgeon. He bred the sturgeons in the fresh springwater of the area, to provide a supply of fresh caviar for his banquets. His guests were offered those precious black eggs in silver cups topped with scales of ice and garlands made of flowers. Of course, only the very best wine would accompany the feast.

- Brasata al Barolo, one of the classic, elegant Piedmontese dishes, is beef slow-cooked in a bottle of very, very good hearty red wine, such as this Clavis Cellatica Superiore. The secret of the taste of the dish is in the wine—the structure and nuances of this complex and refined wine are imparted into every cell of the roast and turn out a flavor and mouthfeel that is luscious, almost indescribably rich and succulent, and worth every penny. Savor it, and the taste will linger in your memory for a very long time. I know it will in mine. This is traditionally and best served with parmagiano polenta, and of course, a bottle of the same wine used for the cooking.

And art? Oh, yes—what marvelous art, ancient to modern, is found here. Eight thousand years BC, the Camuni people of the Valcamonica valley produced beautiful stone carvings, some three hundred thousand of which are now protected in a park. There is the Museum of Santa Giulia in Brescia, with the exceptional Croce di Desiderio (the Cross of Desire), a rare eighth-century masterpiece by a Lombardy goldsmith; the Stradivari Museum in Cremona; and of course Leonardo Da Vinci's *Last Supper* in the convent of Santa Maria delle Grazie in Milan.

Of more modern vintage, the Cà del Vént Vineyard is regarded as one of the most important open-air museums of contemporary art in all of Europe. There are sculptures by many renowned artists. The works are planned specifically for the place they will reside and are installed by the artists themselves. The winery's labels reflect some of the collection's most representative pieces—this wine takes its name from the work *Clavis* (key) by Claudio Parmiggiani, which is pictured on the label.

I feel like I'm taking home a treasure, and I envision sharing this Cellatica Superiore with a worthy inamorato.

**DESCRIPTION:** Cà del Vént Clavis Cellatica Superiore is a unique blend of six different grapes, produced only in those years when the grapes are the very finest. The vineyards are hand-cultivated, the grapes are hand-harvested, and only the best are selected for this wine. Each variety of grape is vinified separately in order to keep alive all the aromas and flavors of the individual grapes.

Two of the varieties used are traditional native Piedmont grapes—Barbera and Marzemino. Pure Barbera wines from the Piedmont are rustic but demonstrate good, round fruit flavors that are easy drinking right when they are released. Blended, the Barbera grape provides a deep ruby color, robustness, intense fruit flavors, structure and softness, and potential for long aging.

From the Marzemino grape, noted for its mention in Mozart's opera *Don Giovanni*, come deep, dark color tones and a light plummy taste.

Schiava Gentile, Incrocio Terzi N1, Cabernet Sauvignon, and Merlot round out the blend, each contributing to the full, smooth, and complex taste.

Combined, the whole is truly more than the sum of the parts—the result is an opulent and aristocratic wine.

First aged for two years in French oak barriques, the wine is then bottled and spends an additional eight years in the Cà del Vént wine cellars developing its elegant and refined character. It is released for sale ten years after vintage—truly a masterpiece of the winemaker's art.

Cà del Vént Clavis has exceptional aging potential. This amazing wine will continue to mature, evolving magnificently for another twenty-five years after release.

**TASTING NOTES:** This is a truly luxurious, elegant, and refined wine. Savor it with all of your senses and explore its depth and beauty to the fullest, like the magnificent art it is.

Pour it into the crystal goblet it deserves. Notice the intense, deep dark plum color, with burgundy-red reflections and highlights as you swirl the glass.

The aroma explodes in a many-layered kaleidoscope of scents—red fruits, cherries, currents and plums, dried fruits and violets, oriental spices and vanilla, hints of dark cocoa and mellow leather.

And the taste—aromatic, elegant, persistent, smooth, and complex—strawberry and red currants and plums, and so many others, reflecting each grape's unique personality mellowed by the magic of the oak and the aging. There are hints of chocolate and spices, warm vanilla, and reflections of the earth and minerals that gave birth to the grapes. This is truly an amazing and sensual wine.

**FOOD PAIRINGS:** Reserve this Cà del Vént Clavis Cellatica Superiore for those special occasions that demand only the best red wine to complement the finest cuisine, especially the foods of the Lombardy region and Brescia.

Make a comforting yet luxurious Brasato al Barolo (beef braised in Barolo, or a similar red wine, like this Cellatica Clavis), and serve with polenta and another bottle of this exceptional wine.

Enjoy it with the best grilled red meats and wild game, perhaps prepared in the Brescia manner known as "spiedo"—slowly spit-roasted.

Try it with a special lasagna or an elegant porcini mushroom risotto. We guarantee a dining experience that will be long remembered—elegant, exceptional, with understated extravagance befitting nobility.

# Franciacorta
## Sensual, Sophisticated Seduction — Inspired by Cà del Vént Franciacorta Brut Saten

**STORY:** Silky… soft… sensual… seductive… sophisticated… simple yet elegant…these words might describe one of those long, sleek satin dresses or nightgowns, worn by those gorgeous and sexy classic 1930s and 1940s actresses as they sipped bubbly and enchanted movie audiences and the leading man. What woman doesn't secretly long to feel like this, to be admired and adored like these ladies were?

I think I might have found the magic potion to accomplish such a transformation…

The elixir that never fails to transform me into a seductive 1930s/1940s actress could well be described by these same words, silky… soft… sensual… seductive… sophisticated… simple yet elegant. Perhaps that's why it works so well. It's the aptly named Franciacorta Brut Saten ("satin") from the Cà del Vént winery. I learned the story of this sparkler from the vintner at Cà del Vént. Come, see if it works the same magic on you.

If you love sparkling wines—Champagne from France, Cava from Spain, Prosecco from Italy, and other effervescent and sparkling wines from other countries—but haven't heard of or tried Franciacorta, this might be understandable.

"Franciacorta"—this single word describes three things: the region, the wine, and the production method—just as the word "Champagne" does.

The Franciacorta region of Lombardy, in northern Italy, is only about one-tenth the size of the Champagne region in France, and its total annual output of all types of wines—reds, still whites, and sparkling wine—is just thirteen million bottles, which represents only about 4 percent of the Champagne region's annual production. Franciacorta is Italy's finest sparkling wine—the best Franciacorta wines are on a par with the best Champagnes. These Franciacorta sparklers are produced using the traditional method, that is, with the second fermentation taking place in the bottle.

Think Champagne is the oldest sparkling wine? "Contrariamente," as my Italian friend says. Effervescent wines have been known in Italy for almost eight hundred years, and if there had been bottles strong enough at that time to withstand the pressures of secondary fermentation, Franciacorta might have arrived on the European market one hundred years ahead of Champagne. But, rather than risk losing their entire cellar to exploding bottles of bubbly, the winemakers of the area decided to focus on their still wines and make them primarily for local consumption.

Production of sparkling wine didn't resume in Franciacorta for almost four hundred years, and then, it was by a serendipitous discovery. In the late 1950s a young winemaker, Franco Ziliani, who had a love of history, found a dusty old book, *Libellus de Vino Mordaci*, written in 1570, on the shelves of the local library. The book described the bubbly wines of Franciacorta. He was inspired and convinced his employer, the prestigious Berlucchi winery, to allow him to try his hand at making a Champagne-style wine, using the process developed by the French monk Dom Pérignon—wines refermented in the bottle, in the method champenois. When Guido Berlucchi tasted the sparkling wine, he was impressed. It was as good as any French champagne, in fact, he felt, even better. The first bottles were released for sale in 1961, to great acclaim. The success of this first release changed the course of wine making in Franciacorta and brought the world another great sparkling wine to light up celebrations and special occasions, and complement the finest meals.

Love Chardonnay and Champagne or sparkling wine that is made only from Chardonnay grapes (sometimes called Blanc de Blanc)? If so, Cà del Vént Franciacorta Saten is your kind of bubbly—100 percent Chardonnay. As with all Franciacorta Saten wines, it is dry, "brut," with a bottle pressure of less than five atmospheres, which is what gives the wine a lovely expression of softness. This is certainly part of its secret allure. When I sip it, I feel a lover's kiss on my tongue—soft, sensual, and tingly electric.

I think this Cà del Vént Franciacorta Saten might just be the perfect wine to serve for a special occasion when you want to invoke the aura of the sensual, romantic, sophisticated, and elegant 1930s and 1940s. I know it always works for me. Just add candlelight or firelight, soft music, crystal champagne flutes, flowers, and dinner or just hors d'oeuvres. Pop open a bottle—with or without that long satin dress or nightgown—and let the magic begin.

**DESCRIPTION**: The Cà del Vént winery and vineyards sit high atop a hill in southern Franciacorta, Lombardy, an area known for exquisite wines and foods. It's a small boutique winery, where art and wine come together in a unique and memorable way.

Like all Cà del Vént wines, Cà del Vént Franciacorta Brut Saten is literally a handmade artisan wine—no machines in the vineyards, all tending by hand. It is 100 percent Chardonnay, with the grapes hand-selected.

The process that creates Cà del Vént Franciacorta Saten is unique and contributes to the elegant and rich character of this wine. Half of the wine that will make this Saten is aged for six months in stainless-steel vats to preserve the fresh, fruity, and floral elements of the grapes; and half is aged for six months in small oak casks for a rich, creamy character. The wine is then transferred to bottles for the second fermentation. All riddling is done lovingly, by hand, over a one-month period. The wine rests fourteen to eighteen months on the yeasts. Then, after disgorgement, the wine is aged for an additional six months in the bottle.

If you are familiar with Prosecco, this is a very different sparkling wine—the taste is far more subtle and complex, the bubbles smaller, more plentiful, and more persistent. Prosecco is made from the Glera (formerly known as Prosecco) grape, and by a different process, fermented in vats rather than in the bottle, and aged only four to five months, so they are usually lighter and sweeter, designed for an informal party or aperitif. Franciacortas are, in contrast, aged even longer than most French Champagnes.

This wine is not meant to be aged, but enjoyed now, or within no more than two to three years.

For serving, I recommend the classic technique of placing the bottle in a bucket of water and ice for about thirty minutes in order to bring the wine to the correct serving temperature of forty to forty-six degrees Fahrenheit.

Serve this pale yellow-gold gem in transparent crystal flute glasses to appreciate the beautiful mousse and perlage.

*TASTING NOTES:* Cà del Vént Franciacorta Saten is truly a beautiful wine. It pours sunlit yellow into your crystal champagne flute, golden highlights glowing in the light. If you are a blonde, it is a perfect reflection of your hair; if you are a brunette or redhead, it will contrast and highlight the gold undertones in your tresses. If you happen to be a more mature, seasoned, and experienced woman, this wine can provide the gold to complement your silver.

The bubbles rise elegantly, sensually; they are very fine and persistent. They sparkle like hundreds of tiny diamonds or stars as they spiral and rise in your glass.

The aroma is intense and complex. There are floral notes of white and yellow flowers, scents of fruits (citrus, apple, and banana), and spice (vanilla, nutmeg, ginger, and anise), and hints of bread and toffee. Luscious...

And the taste—creamy, intense, full, and rich, with the flavors echoing the nose. You may also taste peach and apricot, and perhaps some grapefruit, followed by melons and almond. It's dry, of course, smooth, and well-balanced, refined, and elegant. Persistent on the palate. The bubbles are creamy, recalling the softness of silk from which comes the name "satèn".

*FOOD PAIRINGS:* Cà del Vént Franciacorta Brut Saten is a rich, elegant wine. Because Franciacorta is richer and fuller, as a rule, than Champagne, it is more versatile and can be served with richer dishes that would overwhelm most Champagnes.

Soft and sensual, it is certainly the perfect aperitif and excellent on its own, but like all Italian wines, it is meant to be served with food—from antipasti to desserts, and all the courses in between.

For antipasti, Saten complements caponata, mild cheeses, foie gras, olives, oysters, and smoked salmon.

We love it with seafood such as lobster with drawn butter, clams, scallops, and most light, white-fish-based dishes.

Try this Saten with lightly seasoned baked pasta or subtly flavored risottos, such as truffle or fresh mushroom, or saffron-scented *risotto alla milanese*, a specialty of Lombardy.

We think it pairs perfectly with vegetarian dishes of many kinds, especially those with fresh mushrooms.

For something different and unexpected, yet delightful, try Saten with the Italian specialty popetta di carne fritta (fried meatballs). Great on an hors d'oeuvre tray!

# Rarer Than a Bentley, Perfect for a Day in June—Inspired by Cà del Vént Sospiri Franciacorta Brut Millesimato

**STORY:** This is the story of wine, a sparkling wine, so special that it could change your life. It's a wine that very few people in the world have an opportunity to savor. If you are lucky enough to acquire a bottle and decide to share it, or are invited to share a bottle, be careful.

This wine is a masterpiece of the winemaker's art, a rare treasure to be shared in the creation of the most elegant and sensual of memories. Its name will give you a hint—*sospiri* means sighs.

It was just before I left for my year in Italy that this story takes place.

Giotto had invited me for a farewell dinner. I knew it would be an emotional evening; I just didn't expect it to be so intense.

This being a special night, he had a cab waiting, rather than his usual motorbike.

His apartment was awash in the glow of dimmed lamps and candlelight, several bouquets of fragrant flowers—stock, gardenias, tuberose, jasmine—perfumed the air, and soft music played in the background.

"I am going to miss you, cara," he whispered.

There were two tall tulip-shaped flutes on the table. Giotto returned from the kitchen with an ice bucket and a bottle of what looked like champagne or Prosecco. He offered it for my inspection. It was, unsurprisingly, an Italian sparkling wine, but a Franciacorta, not a Prosecco.

"Jean-Luc and Catherine recommended this," Giotto said. "See, it's from the same winery as that wonderful aged Chardonnay we had at the wine club a few months ago."

I looked at the label: *Cà del Vént Sospiri Franciacorta Brut Millesimato.*

"It's a wine that is as special as you are," Giotto said. He opened it carefully, almost reverently, easing the cork out with an erotic sigh.

He continued, "This Sospiri Franciacorta is rarer than a Bentley—about five to seven thousand of those are made in a year. It's almost as rare as a handmade Morgan Motor Car—there are only eight hundred of those made each year. This wine is handcrafted to the same level of perfection. Cà del Vént produces only about twenty-three hundred bottles of Sospiri in each select vintage year. It is the best of the best, a taste of luxury worthy of nobility..." His voice trailed off.

I raised the flute. A stream of tiny bubbles rose in the glass, sparkling silver against the gold liquid. The wine smelled of flowers, tropical fruit, and spices. I sipped. It was complex and sensuous, with layers of honey, fruit, and spice.

Dinner was equally lovely and sensuous—oysters with prosecco mignonette, figs stuffed with a foie-gras mousse, succulent pan-seared scallops, salad with butter lettuce and avocado. Did I read somewhere that all these foods are reputed to be aphrodisiacs?

The Franciacorta was a perfect complement to our meal and the evening that followed. While a lady will never reveal the details of an intimate engagement, I will say that this magnificent wine was the perfect libation to accompany the perfect meal, and the perfect consummate acknowledgment of a very special and passion-filled relationship.

Just as Franco Ziliani and Guido Berlucchi changed the course of wine making in Franciacorta when they created a world-class sparkling wine in the late 1950s, you might change history in your own life when you share a bottle of Cà del Vént Sospiri Franciacorta Brut Millesimato, whether it's a special celebration or an intimate dinner for two that calls for a most elegant, sensual, and refined sparkling wine, to enhance and be enjoyed with equally elegant and refined food.

No, Giotto didn't ask me to marry him that night. And of course, I didn't cancel my trip to Italy to stay in his arms. But some things certainly did change. I really was going to miss him, after that particular evening, much more than I had thought I would.

**DESCRIPTION:** Wine and art come together at the Cà del Vént vineyard. The name (and label of) Sospiri comes from a piece of art installed on the property by the great Italian artist Antonio Trotta: sculpted from three different Carrara white marbles, the sculpture shows leaves curved by the breeze flowing from the valley, representing the lightness and the delicacy of the Franciacorta sparkling wine. This piece of art is fixed on the main wall where all the Franciacorta sparkling wines are stacked for aging.

Like all Cà del Vént wines, Cà del Vént Sospiri Franciacorta Brut Millesimato is literally a handmade artisan wine—no machines are used in the vineyards; they are lovingly tended by hand. It is 100 percent Chardonnay, with the grapes hand-selected. It is produced only in the best "vintage" years. The term *Millesimato* indicates that the sparkling wine is produced with wines obtained from grapes of a single harvest, called "millesimo." The wine is fermented in new oak casks for at least twelve months, which imparts vanilla, butter, and honey notes. After bottling, each bottle is turned by hand a quarter turn, every day for twenty-eight days. It is then bottle aged for at least forty-eight months. The result is a unique Franciacorta, structured, full-bodied, intense, and persistent—a wine for big occasions, and especially fine with haute cuisine seafood.

There is no other sparkling wine or Franciacorta quite like this—most are known for their freshness, lemon notes, and high acidity, whereas this Cà del Vént Sospiri Franciacorta Brut Millesimato is made seeking great complexity and body, aged much longer than most French Champagnes.

**TASTING NOTES:** Cà del Vént Sospiri Franciacorta Brut Millesimato should be served at a temperature of forty-two to forty-six degrees Fahrenheit, in a tulip-shaped glass, so you can appreciate the brilliant deep golden color— truly warm, sensual summer sunlight captured in a glass—and the complex aromas and taste. This shape also enhances that most captivating aspect of sparkling wines—the bubbles. The mousse is full and firm, the bubbles small and extravagant and lasting.

Like most special things, Cà del Vént Sospiri Franciacorta Brut Millesimato should be slowly savored. Take time to appreciate all the complex layers of aromas, and then tastes. Close your eyes, inhale, and perhaps compare notes with those lucky enough to be sharing this special sparkling wine with you. Do you detect white floral aromas full of ripe tropical fruits, with hints of vanilla, coconut, cinnamon, and nutmeg, enriched with candied fruit, honey, coconut, caramel, dried apples, tea leaf, marmalade, grapefruit, and smoky notes?

The bouquet carries over to the taste—crisp, intense, and complex, with great depth and structure—a truly elegant wine. You will taste ripe fruit, flowers, oak, vanilla and honey, coconut and cinnamon, perhaps melon and apples, perhaps a hint of wood smoke. It fills the mouth—persistent, creamy, elegant, smooth, rich, and complex.

**FOOD PAIRINGS:** Cà del Vént Sospiri Franciacorta Brut Millesimato is a wine meant to be drunk with food. Oh, yes, it's so luscious, you can enjoy it alone, like a Prosecco or Champagne or other sparkling wine, but it is at its best with food.

To truly appreciate this wonderful sparkling wine and create a wonderful, memorable dining occasion, try it with shellfish, seafood, cheese, and even meat.

It matches perfectly with foie gras, duck breast, or ripe cheese.

It pairs exceptionally well with the butter-rich dishes of Lombardy, like saffron-scented *risotto alla Milanese*, or well-fatted osso buco.

With the region's air-cured beef called bresaola and a morsel of Grana Padano or robiola cheese, there is nothing better.

For a special romantic Valentine's Day meal, shape scallops into hearts, crust with curry, pan sear, and garnish with a fresh salsa of diced tomato, chopped fresh basil, olive oil, and balsamic vinegar—heavenly! Finish with dark, delectable chocolate, of course.

# *Region: Veneto*

**Wines:**
    Prosecco
    Prosecco di Valdobbiadene
    Superiore
    Sparkling Rosé Brachetto
    Blend

**Wineries:**
    Rive Dei Frati

# *Veneto*

Ah, Veneto!

Veneto, in northeastern Italy, stretches from the Adriatic Sea, with its golden beaches, to the Dolomite Mountains in the north, offering breathtaking scenery rivaling the Swiss Alps, with tiny picturesque villages and internationally famous ski resorts like Cortina d'Ampezzo, the "Pearl of the Dolomites."

Its cities are as varied as its landscape. There are walled cities, complete with moats, such as Soave, that transport you back in history. Near alpine Lake Garda, medieval Verona is known as the setting of Shakespeare's *Romeo and Juliet*. Vincenza is a mecca for lovers of great architecture. And then of course, there is Venice, the regional capital, famed for its canals, Gothic architecture, and Carnival celebrations. Venice can be garishly touristy, but if you get away from the main tourist hot spots, you will find it to be as romantic and tranquil as it was centuries ago.

The one single dish that is more or less common to the entire region is *polenta*: a yellow or white, soft or thick blend of crushed cornmeal that has been a staple in diets since Roman times. It may be served with fish along the Adriatic coast, or with typical salami and vegetables in the countryside, cooked in wine in Verona, whipped with butter or kneaded as gnocchi in the mountains, or accompanying white or red grilled meat in the hill zones. Venetian dishes make use of humble ingredients and are marked by flavors not particularly strong, but rather nuanced and subtle. The cuisine of Veneto combines simplicity and charm with authenticity and magnificence, highlighting above all the pleasure of little things.

Veneto is best known for its white wines, especially Soave and Prosecco. The eastern part of Veneto, between the hills of Treviso, the plain of Piave River, and the Adriatic coast, is the home of Prosecco.

# Prosecco
## Soft, Sexy, Sensual, Seductive, and So Easy to Love

*In water one sees one's own face; but in wine one beholds the heart of another.*

—OLD PROVERB

Ah, Prosecco, the traditional aperitif throughout Italy, and especially in Veneto and its premier city, Venice. Prosecco is *not* always sweet! Like champagne, it can be made from sweet—"Sec"—to dry—"Brut."

Prosecco, originally labeled "Champagne Italiano," was first made in the Prosecco region of Veneto, Italy, about 150 years ago, from the Glera grape (until 2009, also called Prosecco, after the region), which has been cultivated since Roman times.

Prosecco is made with the Martinotti-Charmat method or *metode Italiano* (developed by an Italian winemaker and associate of Louis Pasteur, Martinotti, and patented/industrialized by the Frenchman, Charmat). The wine undergoes secondary fermentation in stainless-steel tanks, rather than in individual bottles, and is bottled under pressure in a continuous process. This shorter, less labor-intensive method has two great benefits—it is ideal for Prosecco as it preserves the crisp, young, fresh fruity flavor of the perfumey Glera grapes, and it keeps it affordable, with prices for Prosecco substantially below those for Champagne. Prosecco is affordable enough to be enjoyed every day, as the Italians do, with decadent abandon.

# *Venice, Harry's, and "Champagne Italiano" — Inspired by Riva Dei Frati Prosecco Gioss*

**STORY:** Paolo and I are on our way to attend a cousin's wedding near Treviso, a short twenty-five to thirty miles north of Venice. And while Treviso is a lovely city, a smaller Venice of sorts, with canals, well, how can we pass up spending some time in Venice? Who doesn't long to go to Venice? It's possibly the most romantic city in the world. Yes, even more romantic than Paris.

We take TrenItalia's high-speed *Alta Velocità* (AV) train from Florence to the Venice Santa Lucia train station. The trip takes just over two hours, barely time to enjoy a drink in the bistro-bar car. We travel through tunnels much of the way through the Apennines between Florence and Bologna. And since the train travels at over 150 mph, the scenery between Bologna and Venice flies by.

And so we arrive in Venice, "Queen of the Sea." Venice was a favorite haunt of European aristocrats in the 1900s and home of that legendary landmark, Harry's Bar, which I've always been curious about. Ever since opening day, May 13, 1931, Harry's has attracted the international and refined clientele that habitually come to Venice on holiday. We add our name to the guest book, which bears the signatures of Arturo Toscanini, Guglielmo Marconi, Somerset Maughan, Noel Coward, Charlie Chaplin, Alfred Hitchcock, Barbara Hutton, Orson Welles, Truman Capote, Ernest Hemingway, Baron Philippe de Rothschild, Aristotle Onassis, Woody Allen, and a host of others. These rich and famous travelers faithfully appeared every evening, at the aperitif hour. Many of them enjoyed the preferred Venetian aperitivo—Prosecco—just as they do to this day. It's also known an *ombrette* or a "pick-me-up," a perfect description.

I explain my fascination with Harry's to Paolo, whose knowledge of American authors is somewhat limited, as we sit at a table in the corner, a glass of Prosecco in hand. "Ernest Hemingway spent the winter of 1949 to 1950 here, finishing his novel, *Across the River and Into the Trees*. If you read this book, you would probably deduce correctly that Harry's was Hemingway's favorite bar. He immortalized it in his writing, setting a number of scenes in this book in Harry's. For example," I say, searching my memory data banks, finally coming up with the right file, "'The Contessa is not at home, my Colonel,' he said. 'They believe you might find her at Harry's.'"

Paolo nods. "Ah, yes," he says. "Now I see. You wanted to be able to imagine the Contessa here, in Harry's."

"Yes," I agree, adding, "and Hemingway as well. We might even be sitting at his table!"

"Yes, I can see the Contessa myself," he says, winking at me, "sipping Prosecco, or perhaps the Prosecco cocktail invented by Harry's founder, owner, and bartender, Giuseppe Cipriani." Now clearly in his element, Italian food and wine, Paolo continues. "It was in late summer, when the white peaches were sublimely ripe, fleeting morsels of divinity, that Giuseppe, inspired by the luscious perfume, crushed a peach, blended the juice with ice-cold sparkling Prosecco, and added a dollop of raspberry puree to create a delectable libation. He christened it 'the Bellini'—because the color reminded him of the sunset in one of his favorite paintings by the fifteenth-century Venetian artist Giovanni Bellini. Today there are many variations of the Bellini served in bars all over the world, but the best are still made with fresh, perfectly ripe white peaches, and of course, Prosecco, not champagne or any other sparkling wine. You must try one. Just ask any Venetian!"

Paolo raises his glass, and I touch mine to it, smiling as we exchange a silent toast to Cipriani's clever and delicious invention. As I sip my Prosecco, I make a mental note to ask for "the Bellini" when it comes time to refill the glass, or at the next opportunity.

Should you want to visit, you'll find Harry's Bar in a discreet stone building perched along a canal just off Piazza San Marco. He created a timeless and impeccably appointed establishment, based on the concept of serving others as you would want to be served yourself. His vision of simple luxury came to touch the souls of people all over the world. You, too, will be treated like royalty. And do try the "Scampi Amoricaine"—it's far more flavorful than any I've had in the United States.

After savoring a Bellini, I asked for and received the original Bellini recipe from Arrigo Cipriani, the son of founder Giuseppe. For your convenience and unmitigated enjoyment…here it is:

Have everything (glass, white peach puree, and Prosecco) as cold as possible.

The proper ratio is one part white peach puree to three parts prosecco.

Use fresh or frozen white peach puree. If making fresh, don't use a blender or food processor, as it aerates the fruit puree. Use a grater or cheese shredder to shred the peaches, and use a strainer to get the maximum amount of juice.

Add a bit of very fine sugar or simple syrup if the puree is a tad too tart for your taste.

Next add raspberry puree, preferably fresh or frozen, sieved to remove seeds—if you have it, just a little! Can also be served without.

Never use yellow peaches! (At least not if white are available; the flavor is different, not as delicate as white peaches.)

The next morning finds us on one of the most beautiful roads in all of Italy, winding our way north from Venice into the Prosecco region. The hillsides, green with vineyards, rise gently toward the Alps, snowy peaks shining in the distance. We pass through Treviso, an intimate, charming, vibrant, and almost poetic city, where canals and rivers wind their way through the urban environment. Treviso is also the home of my favorite dessert, tiramisu.

We find the old estate, just a few miles from Treviso, that is hosting Paolo's cousin's wedding and reception. The setting is idyllic, enchanting. There is a Bellini bar and ice-filled copper tubs brimming with one of the local Proseccos, a Riva Dei Frati Prosecco Gioss, for "purists." I try a Bellini, which is truly luscious, although not quite as perfect as the one last night at Harry's. So I later shift to Prosecco to better complement the food—all local specialties—prosciutto-wrapped melon, marinated seafood salad, fried crab claws, anchovies with egg, tiny octopus, polenta, creamed cod, risotto with peas and asparagus, soft cheeses, and those famous purple artichokes. For dessert, tiramisu, of course, and wedding cake, and that light, refreshing classic—sgroppino—a scoop of local lemon sorbetto in a glass of, you guessed it, prosecco.

I think there is no better way to end the day, and begin the night, than with good friends and a luscious, fruity sparkling wine, like that Riva Dei Frati Prosecco Gioss. No matter where I am, it always takes me back to Venice and the weekend trip north into the Prosecco wine region for that fairy-tale wedding. As they say in Venice, "Any day is a good day for Prosecco." And I might embellish that a little and add, "Any day is a better day with Prosecco."

**DESCRIPTION:** This particular delightful Italian sparkler from Riva dei Frati is extra dry, with a wealth of tiny bubbles and a lovely, fresh fruity taste. As the label indicates, it's from the Treviso province. This winery specializes in sparkling wines, and they do a masterful job, as demonstrated by this Gioss Prosecco Treviso.

Prosecco is less complex than French Champagnes, which may be one of the reasons for its popularity as a daily aperitif. It is beautifully fresh and fruity, sassy and sexy, meant to be enjoyed young, and affordable enough to be enjoyed every day, with decadent abandon. Serve nicely chilled, forty to forty-five degrees Fahrenheit, in chilled champagne flutes.

With its fresh, fruity scent and taste, Prosecco is not only a perfect aperitif, but also the bubbly to use when making the famous Venetian cocktail, the Bellini, or another favorite Venetian aperitivo, the Spritz, which combines Prosecco, Aperol or Campari, and soda. This simple Italian cocktail is *the* drink for summer: three parts Prosecco, two parts Aperol or Campari, one part soda, over ice, garnished with an orange slice.

**TASTING NOTES:** Poured into a tall champagne flute, Riva Dei Frati Gioss extra-dry prosecco glows a soft straw color. Small bubbles rise in celebration to the surface, ready to amuse your tongue. Its bouquet is that of late summer—a fruity scent of peach, apple, and pear, with a hint of citrus fruits. The taste is light, yet surprisingly intense, crisp, and clean. There are subtle notes of crisp golden apple and overtones of peaches, citrus, and honey, with a soft, dry finish.

**FOOD PAIRINGS:** Prosecco is the perfect aperitif, especially lovely ice-cold on a warm summer evening, shared with good friends.

It blends well with appetizers, light meals, and desserts. We especially like it with prosciutto-wrapped melon. The salty, sweet, juicy play on fresh and cured is an exotic dance when paired with bubbly Prosecco. Your palate will feel like it's on a tour of tastes and textures.

Try it with delicately flavored seafoods, such as crabmeat or calamari, and light citrus salads with lemon—notes of honeysuckle, melon, green apple, pear, and toasted almond can be drawn out with the right vinaigrettes and sauces.

For something very special, try it with oysters, especially oysters with Prosecco Mignonette. The acidity of mignonette sauce unlocks the bright flavors of fresh, briny oysters, and topping off the sauce with Prosecco adds a hint of sweetness—and some bubbles, of course!

The fresh taste and lively bubbles are also a great counterpoint to rich pasta with a white sauce, or grilled calamari or paella.

At the end of a summer meal, if you're not having sgroppino (or even if you are!), this extra-dry sparkler is delightful with crisp, buttery cookies and fresh, juicy fruits.

# How to Add the Romance of Venice to Your Life—Inspired by Riva Dei Frati Prosecco di Valdobbiadene Prosecco Superiore

**STORY:** Paolo's cousin's wedding and reception in Treviso over (wow, does she ever know how to pick a location!), Paolo and I are back in Venice for a little romance of our own. My historical and literary curiosity about the famous Harry's Bar having been assuaged by our previous visit, we can now sample some of Venice's other, perhaps more romantic, delights. And I know there will be more Prosecco in our immediate future.

If there was ever a wine for all seasons, all reasons, all occasions (or no reason or occasion, other than "it's Tuesday"), this is it. Prosecco, the sexy, seductive, sensual, easy-to-love Italian sparkling wine. You can enjoy it any time, any place: it defines informality yet is surprisingly elegant. A glass brings added pleasure to anything it is paired with, and it also does wonders to smooth out the bumps in life's sometimes rocky road. Italians, who know a thing or two about wine and the pleasures of life, drink it all the time—it in the afternoon at cafés, before dinner, and at celebrations such as weddings and birthdays. In fact, no self-respecting Roman or Venetian would go out to dinner without first having a glass or two of Prosecco.

Some of the best Prosecco comes from Valdobbiadene and is classified as "Superiore." A tall flute of this prosecco is simple: visually perfect. The color is that of pale, straw-colored crystal, with strings of tiny bubbles rising like miniature pearls to the surface. And the taste—we are reminded of the words attributed to Dom Pérignon: "Come quickly; I am drinking the stars!"

It's late afternoon, the day fading into night. We step into a gondola. Paolo holds a bottle of Riva Dei Frati Prosecco di Valdobbiadene Superiore, conveniently chilled. And then, he magically produces two champagne flutes. "How does he do this?" I wonder and quietly sigh.

Imagine that evening: the soft splash of a gondola plying a watery back-street, the pink-and-orange sunset flaring and then fading into the indigo night, the stars a spray of tiny, brilliant diamonds. A well-iced bottle of

Prosecco appears, two frothy glasses are poured, two eager hands lift them to awaiting lips, two eager mouths taste, and two lovers almost simultaneously exhale a satisfied "Aaahhhh." Because this moment is *so* good—they both lightly embrace, look deeply into each other's eyes, smile, and say, as if rehearsed, "Gooood," the way the Latino soccer broadcasters draw out the vowel and say, "Gooooal!"

"Yes," I think, "I am drinking the stars, the stars on a warm summer night, with soft, cool sea breezes caressing my lips and tongue."

Light, mildly citrusy with a hint of pear and perhaps ripe melon, it is simply, uncomplicatedly enjoyable in a way that, in these circumstances, not even Champagne could be: the perfect wine in this magical place and time.

Much later, we are at the tiny Alle Testiere, so intimate that we easily stay wrapped up in each other, despite close-set tables. And the food is excellent. Since we are among the last to be seated, we can linger lovingly over a voluptuous dessert. Dinner includes swordfish carpaccio, scallops with orange and Cervere leeks, potato gnocchetti with small calamari and cinnamon scent, and a mixed grill of fish and crustaceans. For dessert, we have *crema rosada*, the Venetian version of crème caramel.

The next morning, we make our way to St. Mark's square early enough to experience a sight that most visitors miss—this magnificent space with almost no one in it, save a waiter here and there setting out tables and chairs. We attend the early Mass sung at the St. Mark's Cathedral, hear ethereal voices soaring to the heavens and reverberating within the domes, and are awestruck by the acres of glittering gold mosaics inside, all without the madding crowds of tourists that will come a little later in the day.

We enjoy a cappuccino at the intimate bar counter at the back of Caffè Florian at piazza San Marco. Then we wander the back alleys and canals of Venice and catch a *vaporetto* to the island of San Giorgio. The view from the top of the bell tower on San Georgio literally makes our hearts soar.

Later, a short stroll takes us to the Ca' Rezzonico at Dorsoduro on the Grand Canal. This is a most unique art museum, home to art that depicts flirting, wooing, sensuous liaisons, and marriage customs in eighteenth-century Venice. "Ah," I think to myself, "culture with a romantic, even erotic, twist!" Paolo and I decide a brief (well, not too brief) respite at our hotel is in order.

Where to spend the evening? We take a *vaporetto* to Giardino, at the lagoon side. We stroll down the Castello promenade to via Garibaldi and perch at one of the tiny tables outside at El Refolo for our *aperitivo*.

Paolo and I engage in a lighthearted debate, "Champagne vs. Prosecco"—sipping Prosecco of course. We agree that comparing Champagne and Prosecco is a case of apples versus oranges. They are two completely different entities. Champagne, for all its festive associations, is often austere, its fruit secondary to its minerality and structure. Prosecco is never austere—it tends to softness, a gentle fruit-forwardness, seductive rather than confrontational, with some minerality after, and plenty of structure if you look for it.

Paolo gives me a devilish sideways glance. A smile plays at the corners of his lips as he says, "Prosecco doesn't demand you look for anything, just that you enjoy what's in your mouth." His smile broadens suggestively, and he adds, "If ever a wine says 'Love me!' it's Prosecco."

I laugh and feel my cheeks warming with a blush, though I don't quite know why.

Paolo continues, "Yes, but this is still a 'real' wine, and sufficiently complicated that one can subject it to a thorough organoleptic analysis, if someone was so minded." He looks at me, with that same devilish smile, and almost whispering, he adds, "But why would you? If ever a wine invited immediate enjoyment—analysis later, if at all—it's Prosecco. Like almost all beautiful, seemingly casual things, that ease and informality results from hard work and great care. Italian winemakers at their best never forget that the highest art is to hide art, to make it all look and taste easy, as if it were inevitable—like the best artists, the best lovers..."

Suddenly, I understand. This Riva Dei Frati Prosecco is a perfect example of this art and always reminds of this truth. A sensuous fire ignites in my mind, and, as I remember passages from Ovid's *Ars Amatoria*, spreads downward through my body.

We have dinner at Ristorante Riviera on the Giudecca Canal, wider and plied more by workaday craft than the Grand Canal but stunning nonetheless.

We enjoy *baccalà mantecato* (steamed cod), buckwheat pappardelle with wild mushrooms and king prawn tails, Venetian-style cuttlefish in black ink sauce over white corn "biancoperla" polenta, lamb chops with lavender, and a zucchini flan. And for dessert, tiramisu.

It's our last night in Venice. We make the most of our romantic escape.

A glass of Prosecco di Valdobbiadene Superiore always seems to transport me back to the romance of Venice with the fondest memories of the time I spent there.

**DESCRIPTION:** The best Proseccos come from a very small area in northeastern Italy with a jaw-breaking name: Valdobbiadene (val-do-BYA-denay). It's a DOCG, indicating the nation's highest wine classification. And this Riva Dei Frati Prosecco di Valdobbiadene also carries the designation "Superiore"—meaning of the highest quality.

The Riva Dei Frati winery derives its name from a small estate that was once owned by Dominican friars, near the charming town of Col San Marino, renowned for its fine Prosecco. Riva Dei Frati specializes in producing small quantities of exceptional Prosecco sparklers, such as this one.

Like all Proseccos, this Riva Dei Frate Prosecco Superiore Dry is made by the Martinotti-Charmat method or *metode Italiano,* preserving the crisp, young, fresh flavor of the grapes. Elegant, approachable, lusciously fresh and fruity, almost everyone will enjoy this sparkler.

Serve nicely chilled, forty to forty-five degrees Fahrenheit, in chilled champagne flutes.

**TASTING NOTES:** This Riva Dei Frati Prosecco di Valdobbiadene Superiore Dry looks as good as it tastes. A lovely, pale straw-yellow crystal in the glass, with a fine mousse and fine strings of the tiniest bubbles— it is elegant and intriguing. The nose is citrusy mandarin orange, with hints of pear, melon, and mineral.

The taste is fruity and slightly floral, fresh, very sensual and seductive. This is a dry to slightly off-dry Prosecco, not at all sweet, so easy to sip, so easy to love. It has a lovely feel in the mouth, and a substantial finish.

One friend, at a tasting, described it as "enchanting, even ravishing, from the first sip…"

**FOOD PAIRINGS:** This is the perfect aperitif on a warm afternoon or evening, the perfect sparkler for weddings and other celebrations, the perfect bottle for a special brunch or a romantic fireside evening.

We love Riva Dei Frati Prosecco di Valdobbiadene Superiore Dry before dinner, and then with our antipasti/hors d'oeuvres. For something special, try it with dates stuffed with Gran Padano, prosciutto-wrapped melon, and fresh oysters on the half-shell, dressed with a Prosecco mignonette for a truly unique hors d'oeuvres platter. The sweet and salty tastes and textures combined with this Prosecco will create an exotic and enchanting dance across your palate.

If you are going to use this Superiore Prosecco in a classic Bellini or mimosa, please do this fine wine justice, and use fresh, ripe, just-squeezed peaches, or freshly squeezed orange juice. Your taste buds will thank you, and you will experience these cocktails in all their original luscious glory, as they were meant to be.

Riva Dei Frati Prosecco di Valdobbiadene Superiore Dry is also the perfect way to end a meal. It's lovely alone, of course, or in that Italian classic, sgroppino (prosecco with lemon sorbetto and a splash of vodka), and it complements desserts and pastries, especially that Italian classic, panettone, or hazelnut biscotti.

# Sparkling Rosé Brachetto Blend
## The Secret to Seduction—Inspired by Riva dei Frati Sparkling Rosé Fra Donne

**STORY:** We've all heard the story of Cleopatra's legendary powers of seduction over Julius Caesar and later, Mark Antony. Yet consider this. What if the tool of seduction wasn't Cleopatra's famed beauty, but a bright ruby-red sparkling wine with a bouquet of roses and violets? And what if it were available to you today?

Whenever I open a bottle of Riva Dei Frati "Fra Donne" Sparkling Rosé, I do so with the knowledge that I am, indeed, letting the "genie of seduction" loose. Let me tell you a story that may help explain the power of this "lover's wine," as it's sometimes called in Italy. It begins over two thousand years ago...

After the death of Alexander the Great, whose empire stretched from Greece to India and included Egypt, another Macedonian Greek family came to the Egyptian throne—the Ptolemys. The most famous of the Ptolemy dynasty was of course the legendary Cleopatra, famed for her beauty and powers of seduction.

In Italy, another empire was growing in power—the Roman Empire. The story of its rise to power, the deeds of gods and heroes and warriors and rulers, has been the subject of many ancient writers. But besides chronicling Roman history, these ancient historians also wrote about Italian wines. One of these was a translucent red wine, from the north of Italy, that glowed like a pale ruby in the glass. This sweet, highly fruity and floral effervescent wine was highly prized. Ancient historians wrote of its seductive scent and distinctive flavor, and its reputation for inflaming passions. Experts now believe this wine was made from the Brachetto grape, which has been cultivated in northern Italy for thousands of years and grows there still today.

It was perhaps inevitable that, eventually, Rome's eyes would turn toward Egypt, and Egypt's to Rome.

In 48 BC, Julius Caesar came to Egypt. History records that he brought Roman wine with him, and it is thought that this reddish, sparkling Brachetto wine was included in his inventory. Cleopatra's brother was on the throne, and

Cleopatra was in exile, the result of a family feud. One evening, Cleopatra slipped into the palace where Caesar was staying. Legend says they shared this wine of passion, and as a result, Cleopatra became Caesar's consort. Caesar reinstalled Cleopatra as queen and pharaoh, and he and Cleopatra remained lovers for the next four years, with Cleopatra spending much time in Rome at one of Caesar's country houses. We might imagine they shared many a glass of their favorite sparkling red wine, and that it continued to inspire their passion, until Caesar's assassination in 44 BC.

Cleopatra returned to Egypt to escape the civil war that followed Julius Caesar's death. In 41 BC, she was summoned to Tarsus, in south-central Turkey, to meet Marc Antony, leader of one of the factions contending for control of the Roman Empire. Cleopatra sailed across the Mediterranean Sea and up the Cydnus River to the city. Queen of Seduction and Symbolism, as well as Egypt, legend says she arrived disguised as Aphrodite/Venus. After docking in the harbor, she entered the city though one of the three gates in the defensive walls, known as the Harbor Gate. It still stands today and is now called "Cleopatra's Gate."

Cleopatra so charmed Antony that he chose to spend the winter of 41 BC–40 BC with her in Alexandria. Four years later, Marc Antony was back in Alexandria and spent the remainder of his life there, with Cleopatra. Legend says that the effervescent wine from the Brachetto grape figured prominently in Cleopatra's seduction of Marc Antony in Tarsus, and it continued to inspire the passionate love he and Cleopatra shared, just as it had with Cleopatra and Caesar.

So, again, let me warn you—Rive Dei Frati Fra Donne sparkling rosé is made in this tradition, from Brachetto and Pinot Noir grapes. It is the epitome of charm, seduction, and joie de vivre, or as the Italians say, *gaudenzia*. With its beautiful red-pink color, soft bubbles that caress the palate, slightly sweet taste, and delicious aroma, it has been described as sensual femininity in a bottle. The name, "Fra Donne," means "among women." Is this an allusion to its popularity with the female palate, or to the secret shared by knowing women of its legendary powers of seduction?

Who knows what might happen when you open a bottle to share? My advice is that you be careful, choosey, and very discriminating about whom you choose to share this with. I speak from experience.

**DESCRIPTION:** This sparkling rosé wine may be unlike anything you've ever tasted. Its liveliness, freshness, and intense aroma make it a distinct and unmistakable wine; not quite as effervescent as Champagne or Prosecco, its softer, persistent bubbles (frizzante) produce a delicate froth. Handcrafted by the Riva Dei Frati winery in the Valdobbiadene area of the province of Veneto in northeastern Italy, this luscious sparkler is made from 70 percent Bracchetto, 20 percent Pinot Noir, and 10 percent Merlot grapes, using the Charmat method, which preserves all the fresh and fruity, floral character of these grapes.

Brachetto grapes are known for being highly aromatic—strawberries, red and black raspberries, and rose petals are the most frequent terms used to describe its sensual, succulent scent. Brachetto sparkling wine is known throughout Italy as the wine of passion and romance.

The Pinot Noir grape contributes notes of cherries and raspberries, as well as sensuality. In France, it is often described as "the most romantic of wines, with so voluptuous a perfume, so sweet an edge, it makes the blood run hot and the soul wax embarrassingly poetic." One master sommelier called it "sex in a glass."

With a history and pedigree like this, Rive Dei Frati Sparkling Rosé Fra Donne will delight and enchant you—the essence of romance, femininity, and sensuality captured in a bottle.

Serve chilled, very chilled, of course!

And please, don't hide this paragon of seduction away in your cellar—it's meant to be drunk young, in the first two years of its life.

**TASTING NOTES:** As you pour your nicely chilled Riva Dei Frati Fra Donna sparkling rosé into a chilled flute, notice the tiny, soft bubbles and pale mousse…and the beautiful deep-pink color. Raise it to the light, and you might catch glimpses of ages gone by—history, tradition, and perhaps Cleopatra herself, who started a legend passed down through the centuries. Or perhaps, as the old proverb goes, "In water one sees one's own face; but in wine one beholds the heart of another."

The perfume of this wine is almost intoxicating, like that of a beautiful, seductive woman—strawberries, raspberries, cherries, rose petals, and perhaps violets.

As you sip, the balanced softness caresses the palate. The taste, slightly but not overly sweet, echoes the aroma—succulent strawberries, cherries, and raspberries, fresh and luscious, as the soft effervescent bubbles tingle and delight your tongue. It's almost addictive, like the kiss of an Italian lover.

**FOOD PAIRINGS:** Riva Dei Frate Fra Donne sparkling rosé is the perfect wine for any celebration. Given its history and the legends surrounding Brachetto sparkling wine as an aphrodisiac, dare we suggest it for a special romantic dinner, or Valentine's Day with chocolate truffles and a dozen red roses? Who knows what will happen?

You would naturally think of Fra Donne as a perfect aperitif, or perhaps to end a meal—and you would be right in thinking so.

It's delightful with fresh fruits, and simply spectacular with a bowl of superripe strawberries, and perhaps some gianduiotti (hazelnut chocolates). I know one gourmet chef who loves it with white nectarine carpaccio with cherry Breton sauce and brown-butter ice cream. Try it yourself—thinly slice the nectarines, laying out the slices decoratively on each plate. For the sauce, use about two cups fresh or frozen red tart cherries, one-half cup dried cherries to intensify the flavor, one and a half cups sugar, and about three-quarters cup water; boil for about five minutes. Use vanilla ice cream if you can't find brown butter. Or thinly slice a nectarine and some strawberries, array on a plate, perhaps add a dollop of goat cheese for an appetizer or marscapone or crème fraiche for the dessert version, sprinkle with basil chiffonade, and drizzle with balsamic vinegar reduction syrup.

For a very different and exciting pairing, try it with something very spicy, slightly salty, and intensely flavored—like barbequed pork ribs or Jamaican barbequed pork tail, or with almost any spicy Asian/Thai or Southwestern cuisine—the bubbles in this sparkling wine refresh and cleanse the palate and cut through fatty or creamy dishes. The sweetness also balances the spices very nicely for a harmonious finish. And it works quite well for a summer lunch of cranberry-almond chicken salad.

An unconventional, creative way to use this Riva Dei Fratte Fra Donne sparkling rosé is to freeze it into a granita (frozen flavored ice) to refresh the palate between courses. Scrape the frozen granita with a fork to make very fine ice crystals and enjoy. Heavenly...

# *Region: Lake Garda*

**Wines:**
    Bardolini Chiaretto
    Valtènesi Chiaretto

**Wineries:**
    Zenato
    Ca Maiol

# Lake Garda

LAKE GARDA IS located in the northeast of Italy, dividing the regions of Lombardia, Veneto, and Trentino—Alto Adige. The large lake is long and slim, stretching from north to south.

Lake Garda is the largest of the Italian lakes and was formed by a glacier during the last ice age, over ten thousand years ago. The lake is over ten miles wide at its widest point and some thirty-two miles long. It has over ninety miles of shoreline.

Traveling the lake takes you from the Dolomite Mountains in the north to the morainic hills and plains of Lombardy in the south. The southern lakeshore is low, rolling land and fairly built-up. In contrast, the dramatic fjord-like northern end is surrounded by towering mountains and cliffs. The richly diverse and devastatingly beautiful landscape is punctuated by many beautiful and historic towns that hug the shore of this gloriously blue lake. These towns have charmed foreign visitors for centuries.

The wines produced around the lake have their own charm and character and are as diverse as the terrior. Wines may be named after the lake, "Garda," or one of the three regions bordering the lake, Lombardia, Veneto, or Trentino, depending on where they are grown and other regulatory guidance.

## Chiaretto

Chiaretto is a rosato or rosé wine from the Lake Garda region. The name means "little light one."

They take their rosé wines seriously here, so seriously that there is not just one but two three-day-long festivals celebrating Chiaretto wines. This is probably because there are two areas that produce Chiaretto wine—one, Bardolina, is on the southeastern or Veneto side of the lake, and the other, Valtènesi, is on the southwestern or Lombardia side.

The Chiaretto festival in Bardolina, known as "Palio del Chiaretto," is held in early May. The Valtènesi Chiaretto festival, "Italia in Rosa," is held a month later, in June, on the grounds of the beautiful Moniga del Garda Castle. Moniga del Garda claims it is the birthplace of Chiaretto wine. Given the history of the Gropello grape from which the "west bank" Chiaretto is made, this is probably true.

While both Chiarettos are lovely wines, they are quite different. Those made on the eastern shores of Lake Garda, not far from Verona, in Veneto, are blends of Corvina, Rondinella, and Molinara grapes; the best known of these pink wines is Bardolino Chiaretto. The Valténesi Chiaretto, made on the western shores of the lake in Lombardia, not far from Brescia, emerges from a completely different microclimate and blend of grapes, mainly a mix of different Groppello varieties, plus small amounts of Marzemino, Barbera, Sangiovese, and/or Rebo. The Gropello grape is one of the rarest grapes in the world—there are only about 300 hectares, or a mere 740 acres, in all of Italy.

The winemakers also greatly vary the time the juice spends in contact with the skins. Those made with shorter macerations (roughly six to twelve hours) are called *vino di una notte*, which can be humorously translated in English as "one-night wines." Longer macerations (roughly twenty-four to forty-eight hours) lead to what are referred to as *vino di un giorno*. The Valténesi Chiarettos are traditionally *vino di una notte,* while most Bardolina Chiaretto is *vino di un giorno.*

While Bardolino wines tend to be more well-known, a Valténesi Chiaretto recently won the title of "Best Rosé in the World" at VinItaly, an international wine competition featuring over twenty-seven hundred wines from twenty-seven countries.

# The Lemon Winds of Lake Garda — Inspired by Zenato Bardolina Chiaretto and Ca Maiol Valténesi Chiaretto

As you may notice, I'm departing from convention here. Because this is the last wine story in this book, I'm going to lead off with the "Description," "Tasting Notes," and "Food Pairings" for both of these Chiarettos first. I thought it more appropriate to end the book with the actual, literally speaking, "end" story, which tells of my return home and my adventure-sharing "gift" to my grandfather.

You'll understand why.

**DESCRIPTION:** Ca Maiol Valténesi Chiaretto is crafted from four grapes: Groppello, Barbera, Sangiovese, and Marzemino. It is named "Roseri" for the delicacy of its fragrance, like rosebuds.

The Zenato Bardolina Chiaretto is blended from 60 percent Corvina, 30 percent Rondinella, and 10 percent Molinara.

Either of these could become a staple at summer gatherings. Like all great Italian wine, these are made to partner with Italy's rich and varied cuisine, with subtle flavors that work in harmony with the food without making too bold a statement. As they say in Italy, wine should be *non impegnativo*, meaning it should not demand too much attention. Both of these Chiarettos are wonderful examples of this tradition. And while they may not demand your attention, they may surprise you and your friends with just how good they are.

**TASTING NOTES:** The color of Ca Maiol Chiaretto Roseri is soft pink with tangerine-peel light reflections. The nose is of elegant floral aromas with hints of tropical fruit, lychee, and mango, with some strawberry and incense. The taste is fresh yet elegant and mellow, a well-bodied wine, rich in flavor of strawberry, black cherry, pomegranate, and spring flowers, with notes of white almond. It is minerally with a lingering finish.

The Zenato Bardolina Chiaretto is a light link, with salmon highlights. The nose is fruity and elegant with floral hints of rose and violet, and perhaps peach blossoms. On the palate, it is fresh, very delicately fruity.

**FOOD PAIRINGS:** Both of these Chiaretto wines are excellent as aperitivo wines, with or without food.

Ca Maiol Chiaretto Roseri is the perfect wine to be paired with lake-fish dishes but also with mushrooms and white-meat dishes that are spicy and structured. It is excellent with fried fish—and a great replacement for beer with your fish and chips, too!

The Zenato Bardolina Chiaretto pairs well with light starters, fish, white meat, seafood risotti, and handmade fresh pasta in lighter, more delicate sauces.

We like both of these with sushi, sashimi, ceviche, or fresh oysters.

Try it with vegetarian dishes, such as avocado-and-tofu salad, for a special summer treat.

For something different, try a Chiaretto with *gzoya* (Asian dumplings) or other slightly spicy Asian or Thai dishes—it's a great match with these foods!

**STORY:** Before I traveled to Italy, my grandfather sat with me, smiling wistfully, remembering happy times from long ago and far away…"You must go," he said, "and visit Lake Garda.

"It is like no other place. There are forty different winds that blow, each with a different name. These create small waves that ripple across the lake; the soft winds gently caress their admirers, as would a beautiful woman running her lithe fingers through a young lover's hair. Sit, as Goethe sat, and as I did, and let dreams of joy and beauty, warmth and pleasure, friends and lovers, wash freely over you, dancing with the wind, fragrant with lemons…and when you come home, please, tell me it is still the same…" He stopped and gazed into the depths of my very soul, his eyes moist with emotion. The quiet of this moment emphasized the importance of what he wished to share, his passion for Lake Garda and the priceless memories inspired by its lemon winds.

He didn't have to say another word. He didn't have to add, "And savor the wine and the food." That I could take for granted. His wish for me was for something much greater, something that should be as important to me as the memories of Lake Garda's lemon winds were to him. I thought perhaps he hoped too that I would find true and lasting love there, as he had so long ago.

That was the situation, and those were the thoughts we exchanged when I was leaving the States for my year-long adventure in Italy.

Now you find me finally back home, sitting with my grandfather. This time it is I who wear the wistful smile.

I've thought about this moment, this time for sharing my adventures with my grandfather, long and hard. Everything has to be just right. I want to capture the spirit of my experiences in Italy and recreate my memories point by point, making my stories vividly real, and bringing the sights, sounds, and feelings I experienced there magically to life in their telling.

I have wine, some bread and cheese, and a plate of simply prepared fish. The cheese and fish are arranged artfully on a plate; the bread is wrapped in a light towel that is lining a woven basket. I intend to serve these as they would be presented, Italian style, at any of the small family restaurants around Lake Garda. I believe I am well prepared, ready to transport us both back to the Lake Garda of our memories and dreams.

To complete the sensory illusion, I have strategically placed a bowl of lemons, one of which I sliced and gently mashed in the bottom of the bowl, on the sill of an open window nearest the chair where my grandfather will sit. I also placed a small Meyer lemon plant, fortuitously found in bloom at a local greenhouse, beside a curtain near the doorway. I've hidden a small fan behind the curtain and plant and set the fan on "low," so as to gently move the lemon-blossom-scented air in the direction of the chair.

I have, in fact, not one, but two bottles of wine open, each chilling in a bucket of ice. I've put a small table beside my grandfather's chair. On it are the plated cheese and fish, the basket of wrapped and heated bread, and four empty wine glasses, two for each of us, so we can sample and compare each wine over the course of the afternoon. I pour our first taste of each wine into our glasses.

"This first one is a Bardolina Chiaretto, produced on the eastern side of the lake, from the Zenato winery," I state proudly, brandishing my glass with sophisticated flair.

"And this one, this is Ca Maiol's Valténesi Chiaretto, from the western side of the lake," I add, first pouring and then sipping from the second glass while pausing to watch my grandfather sample his. I am delighted to see him smile and nod as he enjoys a second sip. I say, "See how different they are," and my grandfather nods again enthusiastically, clearly enjoying the moment.

I explain a little about each wine as Grandfather continues to nod, taking carefully measured moments to swirl, sniff, and sip.

I sit down now, next to him, take another sip of wine, close my eyes, feel the caress of the breeze, and revel in the scent of the lemon trees. I hate the thought of speaking, of letting go this precious moment. But I know I must begin to tell my story, to try to conjure up the perfect words to evoke the magic in my memories, hoping not to disappoint or bore my grandfather with descriptions too detailed or too dry.

I've chosen my opening lines carefully. I've decided to stay absolutely true to his original request, remembering word for word what he had asked. Certain that he will remember too, I carefully start by saying, "Yes, Grandfather, the winds are still blowing, and olive and lemon groves still dot the hillsides around Lake Garda. The faint green scent of the olive trees and sweet scent of the lemon-tree blossoms still perfume the air.

"Paolo and I visited several of the towns along the shores of the lake. We drove along both shores, the east and the west." I stop and blush, not sure how much my grandfather may have deduced about my relationship with Paolo over the past year from my letters and phone calls.

As my cheeks warm, I worry that my grandfather may notice my blush, so I rush to continue. "One of our favorites on the eastern shore was the medieval village of Torre del Benaco. The old town is still surrounded by medieval walls and towers. It has a lovely little harbor and a museum in the old restored castle there that tells the story of the area's fishing and the lemon gardens. We had a lunch of lake fish, with a local Bardolina Chiaretto, in a little trattoria over-looking the lake and the harbor and castle—here, look." I hand Grandfather several photos. He smiles and says, "Yes, yes, it's the same view as when I was there, all those years ago."

"And on the western shore, there were two towns that captured our hearts—Moniga del Garda and Gargnano," I continue.

"Moniga del Garda is the birthplace of Chiaretto wine. Maybe you knew that? There is a wide and long pebble beach and a tenth-century fortress. I wish we could have gotten there for the Italia in Rosa festival," I sigh. "It's held on the castle grounds, which spread across a hill overlooking the town and the lake, and there are over one hundred Chiarettos to be sampled.

"Gargnano is a larger town, which cascades down the mountainside to end at the lake. It's full of art and history, historic villas, palazzos, beautiful churches. It may be bigger, a bit more populated, and busier than you might remember. But the town is beautiful, as I'm sure it was when you were there. There is just a small beach, and not even a continuous promenade along the water's edge. Ah, but there are restored lemon houses, which more than compensate.

"Did you know D. H. Lawrence stayed in Gargnano while writing his book *Twilight in Italy*? And Winton Churchill visited several years after the war. He loved to come to Lake Garda and paint." I pass a small framed print of a Churchill painting to Grandfather. I know he admired Churchill. He smiles, studying the picture. "I think he was a better prime minister than a painter," he chuckles, "but that's just my opinion."

"We met a man there, Fabio Gandossi, whose family restored and tends *Limonaia la Malora*, a centuries-old citrus grove in Gargnano. He told us, 'For us, the cultivation of lemons is a part of our history.' He said that local lore has it that the lemons grown in that area were once so prized that Russian tsars had them specially imported.

"Fabio explained that the cooler northern temperatures result in bracingly sour fruits with exceptionally fragrant zest—perfect for limoncello. However, it is so cool that they must graft the lemon trees onto sour-orange rootstock to improve the hardiness, and also, once frost threatens, he and his father have to cover the lemon-house structures with glass to create a greenhouse to prevent the lemon trees from freezing and dying."

I become aware that I am talking more rapidly now, gaining excitement in the telling of my adventures as I move along. For an instant I find myself thinking, "Slow down!" But then I decide, no, I'm getting excited because I'm reliving the excitement I actually felt while I was there. This is the real thing! I should be excited! And I should want to share this excitement with Grandfather. I'm just going to go with it.

"Fabio makes limoncello from his lemons. It was so very different from what I was used to here in the States—Fabio's was subtly sweet, perfumed with sunshiny citrus, not at all cloying, and not neon yellow. He said it's simple to make—just water, sugar, and ninety-four percent grain alcohol infused with the slivered lemon zest, but it must be made from the best lemons, the ones from Lake Garda. He uses about a dozen of his lemons for every quart of liquid."

I smile and place a bottle of Fabio's limoncello on the table. "For you, Grandfather."

I can see from the breadth of his smile and twinkle in his eyes that this brings back very fond memories for him. My grandfather's eyes start misting over. "I haven't tasted this since my time in Italy."

He pauses for a moment, lost in a memory. "Yes, I remember drinking limoncello just like this with your nonna, Sophia, when we were young and so in love."

He takes another long and thoughtful sip.

We continue talking and reminiscing. As we eat and sip our two Chiarettos, we debate the merits of each. I'm partial to the Ca Maiol, I think, but it's hard to decide. I really like each of them. This, I reflect, is perhaps an apt analogy for my current romantic dilemma. Giotto or Paolo? Paolo or Giotto? Or perhaps there is someone else, whom I have yet to meet?

That thought births a question I feel compelled to ask. Without thinking further I blurt out: "How did you know that Sophia was 'the one,' Grandfather? The one that you were meant to spend your life with?"

As soon as the words tumble from my lips, I feel a twinge of embarrassment. I did not mean to open up a dialogue about my love life with my grandfather, but I fear that I have just done so.

I need not have worried. It makes perfect sense to him that I should have asked. It must be clear to him that I too experienced the romantic charm of Lake Garda, much as he did. My question is, no doubt, a common one for anyone who experiences the magically romantic lemon winds of Lake Garda.

"Ah, cara mia," he says, "it's like this limoncello. When it is the real thing, you will know. What went before, which you may have wondered if it was true love, will become just an imitation, a shadow. When it is real love, your heart will know."

He takes another sip of limoncello and cradles the half-full glass in both hands. His eyes gaze off into the distance, out the open window by his chair. The subtle scent of lemon surrounds us. The taste of limoncello is still fresh upon the tongue. I sit in silence, enjoying this shared reverie, certain that his thoughts are of his darling Sophia, strolling arm in arm along a flowered path, caressed by the lemon winds blowing softly across the pristine waters of Lake Garda.

# Author Bio

ELIZABETH CALHOUN LOVES traveling and enjoying good food and wine. She has worked and lived in more than twenty countries, including Italy. With her husband and their Italian mastiff, she lives a life of adventure, passion, and happiness.

Made in the USA
Columbia, SC
28 August 2017